SILK PAINTING
for Fashion and Fine Art

SILK PAINTING
for Fashion and Fine Art
Techniques for Making Ties, Scarves, Dresses, Decorative Pillows, and Fine Art Paintings

SUSAN LOUISE MOYER

WATSON-GUPTILL PUBLICATIONS/NEW YORK

Front cover:
UNTITLED. © Susan L. Moyer

Page 1:
SCARF DRESS. © Susan L. Moyer. Photo by Horizon Studios

Page 2:
UNTITLED. © 1989 Ina Kozel

Page 14:
FRINGE SCARF. © Susan L. Moyer

Page 80:
UNTITLED. © Susan L. Moyer

Edited by Alisa Palazzo
Designed by Dale E. Moyer
Graphic production by Ellen Greene

Copyright © 1995 Susan Louise Moyer
First published in 1995 in the United States
by Watson-Guptill Publications,
a division of BPI Communications, Inc.,
1515 Broadway, New York, N.Y. 10036

Library of Congress Cataloging-in-Publication Data

Moyer, Susan Louise.
    Silk painting for fashion and fine art : techniques for making ties, scarves,
dresses, decorative pillows, and fine art paintings / Susan L. Moyer.
       p.   cm.
    Includes index.
    ISBN 0–8230–4831–4 (pbk.)
    1. Silk painting. 2. Textile painting. I. Title.
TT851.M69 1995
746.6 — dc20   95–22731
                                         CIP

Printed in Malaysia

First printing, 1995

1 2 3 4 5 6 / 00 99 98 97 96 95

TO SARAH LOUISE AND HEIDI JEANNE

Acknowledgments

My deepest appreciation goes to the artists whose silk creations are included in this book. I would also like to thank all the students who participated in my workshops for their enthusiasm and insightful questions.

I am indebted to Elin Noble and Don Wiener for their insights into the chemistry of acid and fiber-reactive dyes and related silk painting products, and to Christine Mariotti, for her support and for connecting me with so many of the artists featured here.

Many thanks go to Candace Raney, for her understanding and cooperation, and to Marian Appellof and Alisa Palazzo, for their encouragement and professionalism. I would like to express my gratitude to my daughter Tina Louise for relieving me of the business (office chores) of silk painting so that I could concentrate on this manuscript. And finally, special thanks to my husband, Dale, for his beautiful book design and photography and for his devotion and friendship.

CONTENTS

DRESS. © 1990 Ina Kozel

INTRODUCTION

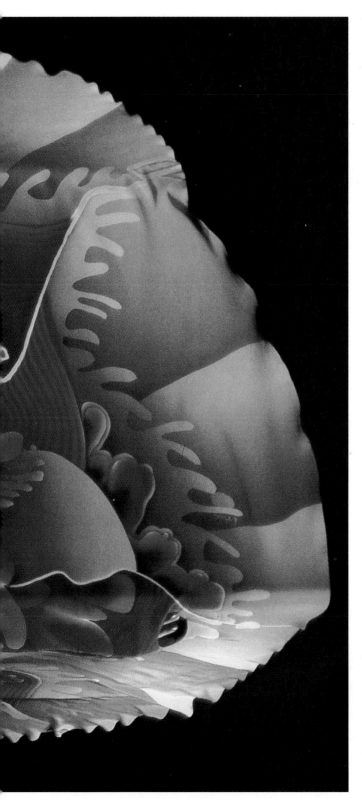

There are many expressive and beautiful objects of art that incorporate handpainted silk. Whether for home decor and fashion or fine art, these different applications require specific materials, techniques, and design considerations.

In my previous book, *Silk Painting: The Artist's Guide to Gutta and Wax Resist Techniques,* I introduced readers to the basic tools, procedures, and enjoyment of silk painting, enabling them to become skilled at, and sensitive to, their craft. In this book, I strive to expand on those techniques and to address how one can embellish the more traditional uses of silk and build ideas for more elaborate projects. I recommend that you read this entire book through first so that when you begin a project, whether it be a painting or a fashion accessory, you can establish the proper foundation to bring your work to successful completion. And, for the readers who are just venturing into silk painting, I suggest that they first practice the methods demonstrated in chapter 6 (Linear Underpainting and Layering Techniques).

My wish is to expose you to the various applications, techniques, and materials available and inspire you to set new, exciting goals. By suggesting flexible guidelines, not absolutes, I endeavor to engage the reader in a dialogue between the technical foundation and creative considerations; therefore, when the reader reaches a goal, the solutions are truly a reflection of his own creative growth. On the following pages, the examples of artistic expression show how completely unique silk painting allows you to be.

As a silk painter, I have a strong commitment to establishing silk painting as a respected, creative art medium, not merely a craft that will soon fade out of fashion. Only through serious effort will silk painting gain the respect it deserves. It has the ability to evolve along with us and reflect the endless potential of our creativity. Just as a medium should not inhibit our creative potential, the evolution of that medium should not in turn be stifled by our lack of commitment to it as an expressive vehicle.

Founded in 1977, the Surface Design Association has championed the art of silk painting and has been a great source of inspiration and knowledge for me and many of the professional artists represented in this book. Another well-established organization is the American Craft Council, which was founded in 1943 and is affiliated with the American Craft Museum, New York City. These organizations have established high standards of professionalism among artists and promote the appreciation of their work by the public. They educate, impart information, and inspire us to greater artistic heights, and their efforts should be acknowledged.

It is my hope that this book might in some way, also inspire you to explore your own creative potential and to share your knowledge and enthusiasm with the rest of the growing silk painting community.

GONDOLAS, VENICE. © 1993 Natashe Foucault

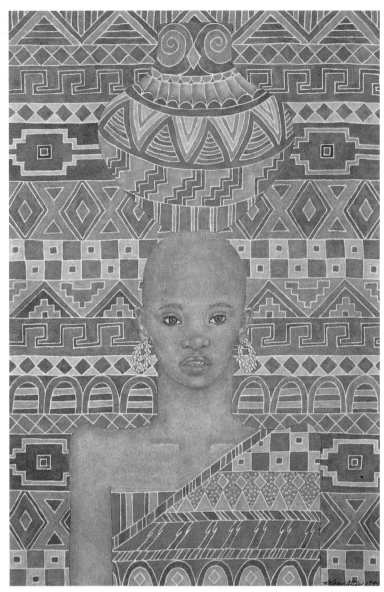

WATER JAR. © 1994 Dolores Littles

RED CAPE. © Marcuse. Photo by Lindy Powers

BROADWAY. © Susan L. Moyer

HORSE. (Silk-wrapped papier-mâché). © Judith Bateman and Suzanne Bateman-Smith

ECLIPSE (screen). © 1992 Betsy Sterling Benjamin

PART ONE: Basic Concepts

Any fine artist must have a good foundation prior to embarking on more advanced methods of creative expression. Here you will find the essential information on tools, color theory, design and layout, and basic fashion projects. Silk painting is a gratifying and aesthetically beautiful means of artistic expression. But it can be even more exciting and rewarding when your creations are useful items that enhance your daily life. With these techniques in hand, you can create fashion garments and home furnishings, as well as fine silk paintings. Each time you prop yourself up on the couch with that painted silk pillow, or don that elegant silk scarf for the finishing touch to an outfit, you will be experiencing your art, instead of simply looking at it.

1 MATERIALS AND TOOLS

For 4,000 years, silk has been prized as a beautiful and luxurious fabric, at once stylish and practical. And for as long as this versatile and enticing fiber has been valued, it has also been decorated. Silk painting procedures have been passed down through centuries of development and from many countries, including India, Russia, and China, and they are still evolving today. This diverse medium naturally lends itself to a variety of projects and techniques, all requiring different tools and processes.

Whether creating a functional scarf or tie, or a decorative pillow or wall-hanging, silk painters, like all artists, must understand their materials: the dyes, diluents, resists, brushes, and, of course, the silks themselves. Armed with these tools and with an appreciation and respect for the medium, you will be ready to explore the exciting uses and creative potential of silk.

DUCK AND FISH. © 1992. Natashe Foucault

SILKS AND THEIR CARE

Silk, a natural fiber, has many applications for the silk painter and is absolutely unsurpassed as a vehicle for vibrant color. The fabric's luster and depth bring luster and depth to the dyes, and its drape is flowing and sensuous. In order to determine a silk's suitability for a specific project, it is important for the silk painter to know the limitations, as well as the attributes, of the fiber and the various weaves in relation to intended techniques and applications.

Silk fabrics are measured in units called mommes (mm), with 5 to 10 mommes being relatively lightweight and 12 mommes and up being more heavyweight and durable. Silk fibers are easily dyed, but the different textures and weights of the various fabrics will affect dye flow, drying time, and color saturation. Dye will flow freely on a 14mm crepe (which is stretchy and durable) or a 10mm habutai (a fairly delicate, lightweight plain-weave silk) because the threads of these fabrics are tightly woven, enhancing capillary action. The dye will flow less easily on loose or open weaves like chiffon because the fibers are farther apart.

You should also keep the fabric weight in mind when choosing a resist; gutta resist, for example, can be thinned to penetrate the smooth surface of a 19.5mm silk charmeuse without difficulty, but it will not penetrate and seal most textured or nubby weaves, which are much thicker. Hot wax, on the other hand, will easily penetrate and create a resist on the more textured and heavyweight silks.

For a small fee, many suppliers make swatch sets of the various silks they carry. As a point of reference, the swatches are well worth the investment. You can test your dyes and resists on them before making a major fabric purchase, as well as pick and choose from among the varieties of silk weaves and weights.

As a garment fabric, silk drapes beautifully, and the weaves and weights of the different textures will affect the flow and line of each piece. It is fairly wrinkle resistant, absorbent, comfortable, cool in the summer, and warm in the winter. Most silks are washable and resistant to mildew and moths, if cleaned and stored properly. On the other hand, silk fibers are weakened by perspiration, antiperspirants, and chlorine bleach. Silk used for draperies and home decor will also deteriorate rapidly if exposed to the sunlight, so treat your silk artworks like fine watercolor paintings or pastel drawings and keep them out of direct light. When stored, silk fabric should not be kept in airtight plastic containers or bags, but rather wrapped in acid-free tissue paper and placed in a cardboard box or cloth garment bag.

Silk paintings can be washed in a nonalkaline detergent, as long as the dyes are set properly. A garment that is made with yards of fabric or is highly or intricately constructed, however, should be dry cleaned to maintain its shape. In some cases, delicately constructed garments should be spot cleaned. Note that dry cleaners use solvents such as perchloroethylene that are referred to as "dry" liquids; this is because they do not contain water, which may cause fibers to swell and shrink and dyes to bleed.

Preparing Silk for Painting

Preparing the silk properly may seem like a more mundane aspect of the painting process, but it is crucial to the success of your final project; poorly prepared silk is difficult to paint on and therefore will result in a sloppy product. Fiber-art and fabric suppliers recommend that you prewash silk prior to starting a project in order to remove any dirt spots that might affect dye colors and also to preshrink the fabric. In this way, you will avoid

These are sample swatches of various types of silk. Available from most fabric suppliers, they are useful for choosing the appropriate fabric and testing dye and resist prior to purchasing your silk and beginning a project.

having your painting or design shrink out of shape after it is steam-fixed. You can use lukewarm water and Synthrapol, a nonionic concentrated liquid detergent sold by many fiber-art suppliers. An alternative to prewashing is to dry clean your fabrics before dyeing; this, too, will preshrink them.

Before you can paint on it, you must measure the silk, tear it to the size you need, and stretch it evenly and tautly on a frame so that it is supported and suspended above your work space. There are a variety of frames available, the most basic being the ordinary canvas stretcher bars that can be purchased in most art supply stores. They are sold in pairs and in different lengths, with two pairs making a frame. Adjustable frames made specifically for fabric painters can be purchased through arts and crafts mail-order catalogues (see the List of Suppliers). You can also construct your own frames using 2-by-4- or 1-by-2-inch pieces of wood and metal corner braces.

Once you cut the silk to the appropriate size, you must secure it to the frame. You can use masking tape or stainless steel push pins for this, as long as you make sure the fabric is stretched tightly so that it does not sag or ripple when saturated with dye. Attach one edge of the silk securely to the frame. Then adhere an adjacent edge next and its opposite edge following that. Complete the fourth side, pulling the silk as tightly as possible.

A luxurious surface to paint on, crepe de chine *is the smoothest and most lustrous of all the crepe fabrics. It is durable and resilient and accepts the dye evenly. The elasticity of the weave gives crepe de chine a beautiful drape, making it a good silk for garments.*

Jacquard *is an elaborately woven fabric that contains motifs and textures in its weave. These patterns can add depth and interest to a design.*

Silk noil *is easily distinguishable from other silks by its natural off-white color, nubby flecks, and rough texture. This texture is caused by pieces of the silkworm cocoon, which remain in the fibers through the harvesting and weaving processes. Dye takes well to silk noil, but the fabric is not as durable as some others because its fibers are very short.*

Pongee *is a tightly woven, plain silk. It receives dye well and is durable and available in both medium and heavy weights. After it is steamed and dry-cleaned, pongee becomes much softer, and its luster improves with wear.*

Charmeuse *has the smoothest, most lustrous finish of all the silks. It comes in a variety of weights and is fairly durable, but it should still be handled with care because the finish can be easily marred. Different types of charmeuse, such as crepe-back and satin-back charmeuse, are distinguished by the weave on the reverse side of the fabric. The sheen of this silk gives added brilliance to dye colors.*

DYES AND DILUENTS

The liquid dyes that work with the silk painting techniques presented in this book have been developed mostly from the acid group of dyes. Certain silk dye colors are categorized as acid, while others are basic, but they are chemically similar in composition and can be used together. To fix (or permanently set) them in the fabric once a garment or painting is finished, and to develop their full color, both acid and basic dyes need saturated steam (see chapter 9 for further information on steam setting). Another type of dye used in silk painting, explored further in the chapter on screen printing, is of the fiber-reactive family. These dyes come in both powder and liquid form and, unlike acid or basic dyes, must be activated with manufacturer-recommended chemicals. They also usually require steam fixing for setting.

Several manufacturers make liquid silk dyes: Pébéo (Pébéo Soie is their line of silk-fabric dyes, *soie* meaning silk in French), H. Dupont, Ateliers Créatifs, and Sennelier (Tinfix and Super Tinfix), all manufactured in France, and Javana and Uhlig, which are German brands. All of these are considered acid dyes (requiring steam fixing) and can therefore be mixed and used together.

Another brand of dye is Jacquard, which is available in the United States. Jacquard Red Label and Green Label Silk Colors are liquid fiber-reactive dyes that differ in behavior and chemistry from the French and German acid dyes mentioned here; therefore, the manufacturer does not recommend mixing or blending them with other brands. The Red Label colors require steam fixing. The Green Label dyes are fixed in a chemical bath made from water and a dye-setting concentrate, and this limits their compatibility with many advanced wax resist and layering techniques. This is because the wax that is used to cover (and save) certain layers of dyes also retards the chemical bath, preventing it from fixing those colors. On the other hand, if you use the Green Label colors along with Jacquard's Water-Based Resist, the dye-setting bath will wash away this resist, thus eliminating steam setting and dry cleaning (which would otherwise be required to remove any resist). This makes the Green Label Silk Colors particularly easy to use. They are most appropriate when working with simple linear resists (listed below).

Silk painters working with the Jacquard Green Label dyes often find it helpful to use a small amount of Jacquard No-Flow. Also called anti-diffusant or epaississant, this clear liquid is brushed directly onto the silk prior to painting or is added directly to the dyes. It helps to control the flow while you are blending and shading colors, and allows for the buildup of textural effects. When using the Green Label colors, make sure they are bone dry before submerging them in the dye-setting solution by going over them with a warm hair drier (even if the fabric feels dry to the touch). Since silk naturally holds moisture, if you don't take this precaution, any damp dye may continue to flow into unwanted areas when the fabric is placed in the setting wash.

Be aware that the more concentrated a dye is, the less permanent (or more fugitive) it might be once it is set in the fabric. Over time, and with extended exposure to both indoor and outdoor light, colors will fade. For handpainted wearable and fine art, where color permanence is important, Sennelier recommends its Tinfix line of dyes. The more vibrant Super Tinfix dyes are highly concentrated to achieve greater brilliancy and are often more fugitive; and even within this line of dyes (as with

Surrounding a Pébéo Soie silk dye color chart are dyes from a variety of sources: Sennelier, Ateliers Créatifs, Pébéo Soie, Javana, Jacquard, Uhlig, and H. Dupont.

other brands), certain colors may be less permanent than others. The Super Tinfix line is really intended for, and favored by, professional surface design studios to use when creating fabric prototypes because the intense hues emulate the colors that will eventually be mass-reproduced on silky synthetics. Permanency is not necessary for these samples, but brilliant colors are. In general, you should test any dyes prior to starting a project, or check with the manufacturer if you are concerned about fugitive qualities.

Also note: When overpainting (layering dyes one over another) with black dye on the more highly concentrated Super Tinfix colors, the black often bleeds past the resist during the steam-fixing process. This happens because black dye takes longer to strike (or set in) the fabric, so it continues to migrate after the colors have already saturated the fibers. To avoid migration, follow the manufacturer's advice and liberally dilute the Super Tinfix colors, especially when planning to overpaint them.

To mix light pastel colors, you must dilute the dyes. The diluent's job is to promote the even flow and application of dye and to prevent the halos of color that often form next to the resist. Most acid-dye manufacturers produce an alcohol-free, concentrated diluent that you mix with distilled water before adding to dye. The recommended proportions of diluent and water vary from manufacturer to manufacturer and are included in the packaging instructions. Dyes can also be diluted using a solution of isopropyl alcohol and distilled water at the following proportions:

• For alcohol with a 70-percent alcohol content, use ¾ alcohol to ¼ water.

• For a brand with closer to a 90-percent alcohol content, use ½ alcohol to ½ water.

When using isopropyl alcohol, always wear rubber gloves and a face mask, and work in a well-ventilated space; the fumes are very strong and toxic, and the liquid is also highly flammable. If you are very irritated by the smell, use a diluent mixed from 1 quart distilled water and a drop of Synthrapol (or a few drops of Ivory Liquid). The soap will help prevent the dyes and the water from separating and streaking when applied to the silk.

Most manufacturers recommend adding 10 percent diluent (either their own brand or your own alcohol mixture) to all colors, and more to obtain lighter tints, black being the exception.

To obtain a rich, even black, do not dilute; instead, apply one or two coats to the fabric at full strength. Alcohol diluent causes dyes to dry faster on the silk, and the alcohol also extends the shelf life of any unused dye solution. Manufacturers' diluents, on the other hand, dry slowly and promote a very even application of dye (especially with tints), making it easier to paint difficult backgrounds or large areas. To get the best of both worlds — faster drying time and longer shelf life, plus an even application — try substituting the manufacturer's concentrated diluent for the plain distilled water in the alcohol diluent mixture; use the same proportions recommended for adding the concentrated diluent to distilled water.

Textural and painterly effects achieved by placing salt crystals and alcohol directly on wet, painted silk in order to absorb and move dye work only when the dye has not yet struck (set in) the fabric. At this stage, it can still be dislodged to create interesting effects. While most of the colors in an acid-dye manufacturer's palette do not strike the fabric upon application, a few of them may, most notably the more brilliant hues, such as bright blues and hot pinks. These and any colors mixed with them tend to set in the silk on contact and streak when applied in broad, flat areas. Remember, too, that in general, the more brilliant the original (unmixed) color, the more fugitive it may be, so choose and test your colors accordingly.

You can often repair streaking and improve dye flow (sometimes referred to as the "wetting out" of fiber) by mixing the dyes with the manufacturer's diluent or adding a touch of non-ionic soap such as Ivory Liquid, Liquid Tide, or Synthrapol. Good for prewashing silks, Synthrapol is also used for removing excess dyes that have not bonded to the fabric fibers. The soap or the diluent will act as a wetting agent that softens and opens up the fibers so they receive the dye more slowly and evenly.

A note of caution: Hygroscopic ingredients (those that hold in moisture) added to dyes to promote fixing, as well as heavy salt residue left from salt techniques, may cause silk to retain a lot of moisture during the steaming process. If the fabric becomes too wet during steaming, the dye may migrate and the manufacturer's diluent or any detergent used may continue to act as a leveling agent, softening textural effects. To minimize this, use diluents and detergents sparingly, especially when overpainting.

Acid dyes are very stable and will last for years. Most manufacturers add a preservative to retard spoilage and suggest that you store the dyes in a dark, cool place so that the colors do not lose their potency due to heat and light exposure.

RESISTS

The primary job of a resist is to control the movement of dye by delineating and separating areas of color, thereby enabling the creation of both figurative and abstract designs. Like the outlines in cloisonné enamelwork, gutta and similar resists are most commonly applied to silk in a linear fashion. The resulting holding lines penetrate and seal the silk fibers, creating a barrier to contain the flow of the liquid dye, preventing it from flowing endlessly over the fabric.

There are primarily three types of linear resists used in silk painting: the traditional gutta resists, which come in clear, black, and colored varieties; clear, water-soluble resists; and pigmented water-based, fabric-paint resists. When choosing a resist, keep in mind that each type has specific qualities, which should be noted so that you use the proper one for a particular project. Read the product labels carefully before purchasing anything.

To ensure that resists will withstand washing and dry cleaning, it is important to follow the manufacturer's instructions. Some resists, the fabric-paint type in particular, require heat setting with an iron. This should be done once the resist has dried, and before the dyes are steam-set.

Resists are quite versatile. Many can be used when screen printing designs on silk fabric (see chapter 8).

Clear Gutta

Gutta is a refined latex product that is derived from a hybrid species of the tropical palaquium tree. Traditional gutta is the resist preferred by professional artists who have developed very painterly techniques. They find that the rubbery gutta resist line will hold up to their techniques, which require repeated applications of dye, diluent, and alcohol.

Once a painting has been finished and the dyes steam-set, the gutta is removed from the silk by immersion in dry-cleaning fluids. Because the dyes used in silk painting are not soluble in dry-cleaning fluids, it is also possible to remove the gutta (by dry cleaning) before the dyes have been steam-set without disturbing the underlying color. Although it is preferable to dry-clean after the dyes are set, there may be times when you will want to remove the gutta or wax before proceeding with a painting.

Gutta is thinned to a working consistency with a solvent. The common solvents used are mineral spirits, naphtha, or solvents marketed by gutta manufacturers. For safety, wear latex gloves when handling the solvents, and keep these potentially flammable and toxic liquids in glass jars or metal squirt containers.

The various resists pictured here include Pébéo clear, black, and metallic gutta; Sennelier clear and black gutta; Uhlig clear gutta; H. Dupont clear gutta; Jacquard and Javana water-soluble resists; Pébéo metallic fabric-paint resists in tubes; and Javana Lining Paint. Also pictured are Kreul and Cres-Lite metallic powders for mixing with Javana Lining Paint and clear gutta respectively.

CELEBRATION OF THE SEA. © Evelyn Jenkins Drew. *Executed with Jacquard dyes, this silk painting illustrates how a white outline (achieved by using a clear gutta) can be beautifully integrated as a design element.*

CUMULUS BEGONIA. © Evelyn Jenkins Drew. *This painting is an exquisite example of the incorporation of a colored resist as an integral part of the design, especially in the linear areas of the clouds and the pier. Evelyn mixes oil-based inks with her gutta and does not dry clean it out of the fabric.*

Solvent containers have a long spout, similar to that on an oil can, which twists open and closed and provides a very convenient way of adding the solvent to a gutta applicator or container.

Black and Colored Guttas

Sennelier makes guttas in several colors, including black. The black version is marketed as permanent and dry-cleanable. During dry cleaning, the gutta will be partially removed and a black line will remain in the silk; however, the line may be a shade or two lighter. Clear and black gutta can be used in the same painting, providing interesting design elements. Sennelier black gutta varies widely in consistency and is therefore notoriously more difficult to work with than clear gutta, but the results are well worth the effort.

The colored guttas (with the exception of black) may be mixed together to produce other colors, but they are not dry-cleanable. You can color your own gutta by adding typographic ink (oil-based printer's ink), but this resist will not be dry-cleanable, only washable.

Black and colored guttas are more effective when applied to heavier silks (12mm and 14mm), which have more fibers. If you are working on lightweight silks (5mm or 8mm), or if the gutta line is applied too thickly, the gutta will become gummy and

---

Tips for Working with Black Gutta

• Always shake the container well before pouring the gutta into your applicator. Black gutta may ooze out of the applicator tip even when in an upright position. It will settle down once some of the gases have escaped.

• Since fresh black gutta tends to be runny, use a small applicator tip, size 3, to control the flow and width of the resist line. If the consistency is too runny, let the gutta sit in the applicator for a few hours or overnight to thicken. If the gutta is too thick, add a solvent and shake the container well.

---

smear because it does not have enough fibers to penetrate and bind to. On clothing, the Sennelier black gutta is also likely to smear when a garment is worn and, during the dry-cleaning process, will lift off the silk and backstain (come off, staining any underlying surface) even after repeated wearings and cleanings. To absorb excess gutta and avoid backstaining when ironing the silk, always iron it between sheets of tissue paper, changing the paper when stained.

CACTUS. © Linda France Hartge and David Hartge. *Linda uses black gutta not only as a linear resist, but also as a means of delineating form and creating textures in her paintings. She often uses black and clear guttas in the same painting.*

Water-Soluble Resists

Water-soluble resists are usually made from a variety of starch and gum thickeners. Water is used to thin them to a working consistency. These resists are a cousin to the rice paste resists used for centuries in China and Japan. They are washed out of the silk with water after the dye has been steam-set. To maintain a good linear resist when painting, do not flood the silk with dye, and avoid alcohol diluents. Some water-soluble resists are marketed as nontoxic and are therefore applicable to many craft projects. But many professional silk painters find that water-soluble resists limit the versatility of the medium, since they cannot endure the rigors of more complex painterly techniques. This is especially true when using overdyeing methods requiring hard-edged resist lines. Here, the repeated application of dye and alcohol diluent will ultimately break down a water-soluble resist.

When water-soluble resists are applied to a painted ground, they will discharge the dye, creating a lighter line of color on the ground. This happens because they contain water and other liquids that disturb the unset dye. Some water-soluble resists need hot water and scrubbing to be removed from the silk, and during this process the painting may lose some color. Also, some water-soluble resists become stiff and permanent when immersed in dry-cleaning fluids, or gummy when put in dye-setting solutions. So, always be sure that your water-based resist is compatible with the other processes you are planning to use.

To achieve a colored resist line, liquid dye can be added to most water-soluble resists. The dye sets in the silk and the resist is washed away. This technique has many applications in the field of professional fabric design.

One water-soluble resist that works well is Avantegarde Gutta Plus (manufactured by Javana). Black and colored liquid dyes can successfully be added to it to create colored resist lines. Note that despite its name, this is *not* a gutta product. Pébéo also makes a water-soluble resist.

Metallic Resists

Metallic resists are available in both gutta-based and fabric-paint forms. Unlike regular gutta, these are meant to remain in the silk. The metallic guttas are not dry-cleanable, however, and over time will flake or rub off the silk. Unfortunately, fabric-paint resists, which are more durable, are usually not pure metallic gold or silver colors and are often not effective resists on heavy-weight silks.

A true metallic gold or silver resist that is durable, washable, dry-cleanable, and suitable for wearable art is a product many silk painters have been asking for. Unfortunately, developing a viable formula has been difficult, because adding metallic powders to resists makes them unstable and thus lacking in shelf life. If you are looking for a gold or silver metallic resist, you might first find the chemist inside you and proceed with the determination to be master of your own materials. You will not be alone. Many fine and decorative artists maintain quality control when working with certain pigments by compounding their own ingredients, such as oil paints, pastels, and gilding materials.

At Galerie Smend in Cologne, Germany, I met Ute Patel-Missfeldt, a popular German silk painting teacher and artist, and the author of several books on the subject. Ute shared with me her method for making a very effective gold metallic resist. She adds a small amount of very fine gold metallic gilding powder (Kreul Bronze powder, 127620 Dunkelgold, which is available in the U.S.) to a resist called Javana Lining Paint. (Javana and Kreul are different divisions of the same German company.) This Lining Paint resist comes in several colors, which, surprisingly, all become metallic gold when the gold powder is added, so any color Lining Paint you choose should work. Ute brings her resist to a working consistency by mixing in a few drops of water. The mixture is stable for about two hours, so she mixes only a little at a time.

The resist can be applied using a resist applicator (see below) or a special liner pen that Ute has designed and developed. The liner pen, which is an adaptation of an old-fashioned ruling pen,

BUTTERFLIES AND THISTLE. © Ellen Shannon. *A charming and stylized image, this piece was executed with gold metallic gutta, which greatly enhances the design.*

permits very even and controlled lines and curves. It is not, however, designed for fluid, freehand drawing. Mixing the resist to a consistency that is compatible with the liner pen takes some skill, but with practice it should become easier.

Even though Javana Lining Paint is marketed as dry-cleanable, Ute finds her metallic liner paint to be washable and durable but not very dry-cleanable. After experimenting with this, I found Ute's metallic liner paint to be resistant to a light dry cleaning. If material and process compatibility are important to you, test them before embarking on a major piece of work.

I was able to make metallic gold and silver guttas by adding a little Cres-Lite Bronze Powder (#601 for gold and #242 for silver) to a good-quality gutta. Cres-Lite is manufactured by Crescent Bronze Powder Company, Inc. Metallic powders come in a large selection of colors and grades of refinement; the coarser grades give more sparkle to the gutta, while the finer grades bind better with the gutta and maintain better resistance through cleanings. This homemade metallic gutta mixture is most effective if used within the first day or two, because fresh resist enables you to maintain a thin, even application on the silk, and it won't flake off as easily as some of the commercial products. Metallic guttas are more durable when applied to a plain weave versus a crepe, since the stretchiness of the latter fabric weakens the resist and encourages flaking.

A note of caution: If you are tempted to explore metallic bronzing powders, which come in many colors, remember that they are made from finely ground metals such as copper and aluminum, which you should avoid inhaling. Wear rubber gloves and work in a well-ventilated area.

Fabric-Paint Resists

I call these "fabric-paint" resists because, once applied, the pigments and binders they contain remain in the fabric, providing an additional, painterly design element. Available in many different colors, some of these resists, like some actual fabric paints, require an application of dry heat to be permanently bound to the fabric. The dry heat is usually applied in a clothes drier or by ironing for a specified length of time, so follow the accompanying instructions carefully to ensure setting. Fabric-paint resists are gutta-free and are usually described as washable and, occasionally, dry-cleanable. Like water-soluble resists, they can also be difficult to use, especially on heavyweight silks. To ensure that a fabric-paint resist will completely penetrate and seal these denser fabrics, you may need to thin it with water. Some artists also put the resist on both sides of the fabric and heat-set it (if necessary) before applying any dyes to be absolutely sure their resist lines will hold.

RESIST APPLICATORS

Resist applicators are small, soft plastic squeeze bottles with metal tips available in various sizes. They offer the control needed to apply thin, even holding lines. Some metal tips have been threaded so that they will screw onto the cap of the applicator. There are two versions of this model; in one, the top screws onto the bottle, and in the other the top snaps into the bottle. The snap-in top has a slight tendency to pop out when the resist is being applied. To avoid this, cut off the very top end of the extra cap that comes with the applicator and screw the altered cap over the snap-in top onto the applicator.

This photograph shows the reservoir of the liner pen developed by Ute Patel-Missfeldt being filled with a gold resist. The instrument is specially designed to provide an even, controlled line width when applying both straight and curved stylized lines. From the book Ute Patel-Missfeldt: Meisterschule Seidenmalerei *(Master School of Silk Painting), Augustus Verlag, 1993, Augsburg, Germany.*

A straight-edged ruler is used here as a guide when drawing lines with the liner pen. Tip: To keep the resist from smearing under the straight edge as you draw, suspend the edge above the surface of the silk by taping two coins to the underside of the ruler. Photo from the book Ute Patel-Missfeldt: Meisterschule Seidenmalerei *(Master School of Silk Painting), Augustus Verlag, 1993, Augsburg, Germany.*

HARLEKIN. © Ute Patel-Missfeldt. Model: Isabel Patel. *In this painted silk cape-like jacket, Ute's design and use of gold shows the strong influences of both Art Nouveau and the culture of India on her work. She uses metallic resist as a strong design element in many of her projects. From the book* Seidenmonde mit Phantasie, *Eulen Verlag.*

HARLEKIN (detail). © Ute Patel-Missfeldt *To achieve the durable, metallic resist required for wearable art, Ute mixes metallic powders with liner paints.*

Other models may need to be assembled by pushing the metal tip up through the end of the applicator from the inside of the cap. To facilitate this, you will need to snip off the end of the small plastic tip. Usually a pin or wire of the appropriate size is supplied with the metal tip for the purpose of preventing the resist from clogging the applicator when not in use. Store the applicator with this pin in its tip. To keep track of these tiny pins and their sizes, make a flag label with colored tape and attach it to the pin.

While most resists are packaged in large containers and should be transferred to a resist applicator for use, Pébéo and Javana have several water-based resists that come in tubes equipped with applicator tips; they can be applied directly onto the silk from the tube. Of course, they can also be emptied into the traditional, smaller applicator, which, as with all resists, makes it possible to add water and adjust the consistency for application.

Also available now is the Silkpaint Air Pen, a recently developed resist applicator with an electric air pump. You activate and control the flow of the resist by placing an index finger over the opening. The Air Pen was developed for silk painters with arthritic hands and carpal tunnel syndrome, who find it painful to squeeze resist through a plastic applicator. You can get small, medium, and large tips that fit the pen and enable the creation of medium- to heavyweight resist lines. The pen is also a useful line applicator for a variety of mediums.

Filling the Resist Applicator
To fill the basic applicator, hold it upright and squeeze in the sides. Hold the open gutta container 2 to 3 inches above the applicator. Pour the resist in a thin stream into the applicator until it is three-quarters full. As you are pouring, if the resist begins to clog the opening, create a vacuum by releasing the pressure you are applying to the applicator sides. The resist will be pulled into the applicator and you can then continue pouring without the resist spilling over the top.

Cleaning and Storing Resist Applicators
Gutta should never be left in the applicator for more than one or two days. The solvent in the gutta will dissipate through the porous plastic, leaving the gutta in a hardened state. To avoid this, either store a gutta-filled applicator in a tightly capped jar of solvent, or transfer the gutta back into its original container. After removing the gutta, lean the gutta applicator open side down against the inside of a small jar or disposable cup to air-dry for a day or more. Once the applicator is completely dry, clean the film of gutta from the inside with a cotton swab, twisting it until you have pulled the thin film away from the sides and out the opening. Do the same with the applicator top. This technique ensures easy gutta removal from a resist applicator. For efficiency, I suggest having two or three applicators on hand so that one can be drying while another is being used.

Water-based and fabric-paint resists don't dissipate or harden as fast as solvent-based guttas; therefore, they can be left in an applicator for longer periods of time, but the metal tip must be cleaned to prevent clogging. The best way to do this is to keep an extra gutta applicator handy. Fill the extra applicator with water and screw on the dirty top. Then shake and squeeze the applicator to flush out the resist.

Here you see several styles of resist applicators and tips, and a solvent (gutta thinner) squirt container. The long thin nozzle on this container facilitates adding a few drops of gutta thinner to a resist applicator.

The Silkpaint Air Pen resist applicator has an electric air pump with which you activate and control the flow of the resist. It was developed for silk painters with arthritic hands and carpal tunnel syndrome, who find it difficult to squeeze the standard, plastic resist applicator.

From left to right are various silk painting brushes and a cotton puff in a wire clothespin. To protect them, you can make a custom brush case out of a reed mat and rows of elastic bands. It can be rolled up for easy transporting.

SILK PAINTING BRUSHES

An artist's creative needs and chosen mediums determine the types and sizes of brushes used. Many different brushes and implements, both new and traditional, are used in silk painting, each with its particular function in the various techniques used to apply liquid dye. Special brushes are also used to apply wax to silk, but these are discussed in chapter 7.

A squirrel-hair quill brush is considered the traditional brush for silk painters because it holds a large amount of dye, comes to a fine point, and moves easily on the silk. Excellent for painting flat color and backgrounds bordering intricate details, it allows the dye to flow freely into the more complex areas of a design, making it easier to apply color quickly and evenly.

Recently, I have been painting with Black Velvet round artists' brushes manufactured by Silver Brush Limited. This brand, which performs beautifully, is a blend of black kazan squirrel hair and Risslon, a synthetic fiber. The combination of the two types of bristles makes the brush much more versatile because the soft squirrel hair holds a lot of dye and moves easily on the silk, while the synthetic fiber adds the bit of stiffness that facilitates blending and shading. The resilient and flexible point assists in controlling the application of dye between resist lines and in small, intricate areas.

When applying colors in large areas bordering nooks and crannies, I use a ¾-inch Black Velvet Oval Wash brush. I refer to this oval-shaped "workhorse" as a background blender. I also paint with small and medium Silverwhite round brushes.

Linda Hartge of Kaleidosilk, whose work is featured in this book, uses a variety of mass-produced brushes but also enjoys working with Keith Lebenzon's handmade brushes. Keith is a professional craftsman who sells his brushes through national craft fairs. His fans consider his unique brushes to be works of art and a joy to own. He shapes each one himself and then secures it in a handcrafted bamboo handle.

Large squirrel-hair brushes are a chore to clean. Many silk painters avoid this task by using inexpensive foam brushes when painting large areas and backgrounds that do not border on intricate designs. They designate one for each color family — plus one each for yellow and black — so they don't require as thorough a cleaning. Another option for spreading a wash of color is to use a cotton puff held in a clothespin.

Quality brushes, if cared for properly, will last a long time. When you are in the process of painting and need to clean a brush, first rinse it in water to remove most of the dye and then in an isopropyl alcohol and water solution. Blot the brush and ferrule (the sleeve, usually metal, joining the bristles to the handle) on a paper towel and continue painting. Once you finish, or if you need to thoroughly clean a brush, swirl it on a wet bar of Ivory soap, or gently work the lather through the hairs and rinse in tepid water. Repeat until clean. Afterward, straighten out any of the center hairs that may have gotten tangled, wet the brush, and shake it into a point. Let the brush dry either suspended or at an angle so moisture drains away from the ferrule and so the brush does not touch a surface, which could cause it to lose its shape.

Never leave your brushes resting in a container of water, alcohol, or dye. The brush will lose its shape, and eventually the handle lacquer will split and peel, rotting the wood. When storing brushes, make sure the bristles are protected from being bent out of shape. Natural-hair brushes must also be protected from silverfish, mice, and other brush-eating creatures, including household pets. To prevent rotting, never store damp brushes in airtight or plastic containers.

Note that certain additional tools, brushes, and supplies are needed for wax resist techniques and screen printing. For more on these materials, refer to chapter 7.

FABRIC STRETCHING EQUIPMENT

When you are painting on silk, the fabric must be suspended above a work surface and stretched taut. As experienced silk painters know, this is not as simple as it sounds. Once the silk becomes wet with dye it naturally loses its tautness and begins to sag and ripple. To keep the fabric from touching the work surface, and the dye from puddling or running into unwanted areas, the artist must constantly readjust the tension of the stretching system in use to maintain control of the sagging.

Other problems are "mark off" and "backstaining," which are industrial terms for uneven dyeing. Mark off occurs when the painted silk dries touching another surface, usually the supporting frame or work surface. Backstaining occurs when the fabric becomes stained with dye that has previously collected on equipment such as pushpins, frames, or the work surface.

Silk painters work on various projects with different types of silk, all having special requirements. Silk cut from yardage, prehemmed scarves, several yards or an entire bolt of fabric, and preconstructed garments all require individual attention to the choice of frame and securing device employed. Necessity being the mother of invention, many silk painters, including myself, develop fabric-stretching devices and systems to satisfy their particular requirements.

Klara Gardon, a now-retired professional silk painter and instructor, suspended her prehemmed scarves above her work surface by lacing elastic, which she wrapped around a frame, through dressmaker's straight pins that she carefully attached to the rolled hem to minimize holes. The self-adjustable nature of the elastic kept the fabric taut during and after the painting process.

Armed with Klara's elastic, I was able to develop and market an adjustable frame and stretching system for fabric and hemmed scarves. The Moyer Design Fabric Stretching System, which is comprised of elastic cord, specially designed rustproof fabric hooks, and cord locks, can be easily adjusted to accommodate both the inconsistencies of scarf sizes and the extra stretch of crepe and other weaves. With this system, the fabric is suspended so it never comes in contact with the frame or work surface below. While the artist works, the system automatically picks up any sagging caused by wet fabric or heavy resists. This adaptable system also enables the silk painter to stretch simple preconstructed garments such as tank tops and capes.

Legs, which slip on and off the frame, can be placed wherever needed so that even a long frame can be supported on a small tabletop. The legs can be removed at any time during the process, so you can trace, draw, stamp, stencil, and screen print a design on a flat surface. They can then be reattached to the frame, again lifting the fabric above the surface for painting.

The frame is hinged so it can fold and stand on end, even with the fabric still attached, making the size more convenient for storing or transporting work in progress. This is particularly helpful for teachers and students who are demonstrating or working on projects at home and in class. The frame can also be completely disassembled for storage and traveling.

Artists like Leo Loomie, who paint large bolts of fabric, have their own sets of problems. In response to his own needs, Leo developed the Dye Tech 60 Fabric Painting Machine, which not only increased his production but lowered the production cost per yard of his original hand-painted fabrics. This unique invention works with bolts of heavy- and lightweight fabrics of up to 60 inches wide, yet is so compact, it eliminates the need for a warehouse-size studio to accommodate the painting and drying processes. It features an exhaust hood to remove fumes, fans to dry the fabric as it is painted, and a foot pedal that controls the speed and leaves the hands free to paint.

Other fabric-stretching techniques can be found in my first book, *Silk Painting: The Artist's Guide to Gutta and Wax Resist Techniques* (Watson-Guptill Publications).

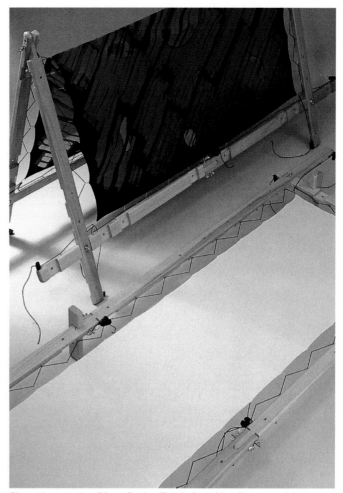

Shown here are two Moyer Design Fabric Stretching System models. A rolled-hem scarf is stretched on the rectangular frame in preparation for painting, while a work-in-progress is in an A–frame position ready for storing. These frames also fold and lie flat against each other.

These are stretcher bars from the Moyer Design Fabric Stretching System, along with a wooden embroidery hoop. The rectangular stretcher frame will stretch silk of up to 16 by 72 inches or 32 inches square. The square stretcher frame will stretch silk of up to 45 inches square. The parts can also be assembled into two smaller frames that will accommodate fabric of up to 18 inches square. Stretcher bars of the square and rectangular frames can be combined to handle fabrics of up to 45 by 72 inches, and multiple rectangular-frame stretcher bars will take fabrics of up to 72 inches square. The embroidery hoop is a handy way to stretch silk for testing materials.

2 COLOR

During the silk painting process, the artist experiences color very intensely. As with many of the visual arts, this natural high is part of the allure of the silk painting medium. Another attraction is the potential for the product of this process—the colorful fabric—to be integrated into our everyday lives not only as art, but as fashion and home furnishings as well. A foundation in color theory will assist the silk painter in analyzing and using color effectively, enabling successful artistic expression whether creating for the textile industry or for personal enjoyment.

BASIC COLOR TERMS

Understanding the vocabulary of color will allow you to identify the qualities of colors; it will also help you verbalize your preferences and perceptions of color, and give you the ability to critique your own work, which is a necessary step toward any improvement. The following is a list of basic color terms. Once armed with this knowledge, you can focus on developing the more advanced technical skills.

A *primary* color is one that cannot be produced through mixing. There are only three: red, yellow, and blue. A *secondary* color is created by combining any two primary colors: yellow plus red makes orange, yellow plus blue makes green, red plus blue makes violet. A *tertiary* color is produced one of two ways: either by mixing two secondary colors, or by mixing equal parts of a primary color with a secondary color adjacent to it on the color wheel. (See below for color wheel information.)

Colors in the green, blue, and violet families are generally considered to be *cool* in temperature, while those in the red, orange, and yellow families are said to be *warm.* Adding a touch of a cool color to a warm one will make the resulting pigment less warm, and the reverse is true when adding a bit of a warm color to a cool one. For example, adding a small amount of blue to red will make the red cooler; adding a small amount of yellow to red will make the red warmer. So, even though red is generally considered a warm color, its temperature is relative—there are cool reds and warm reds.

Complements are any two colors that lie directly opposite each other on the color wheel, such as yellow and violet or red-orange and blue-green. These combinations (or harmonies) are often found in nature—for example, violets with their yellow centers, or a blue iris with an orange center, or red apples growing in (green) trees. *Analogous colors* are three to five contiguous colors on the color wheel, such as violet, blue-violet, blue, and blue-green.

A *hue* is the descriptive name of a color, such as orange, blue-violet, yellow-green, or brown. Mixing any two hues together will create a new hue; for example, red combined with blue will produce violet, and orange combined with yellow will produce a deeper yellow (or a lighter orange, depending on how you look at it). You can also mix three hues together to achieve a desired new color. Adding a fourth hue will most likely create too muddy a color, so take care when mixing.

Value is the lightness or darkness of a hue in relation to white and black, and it can be altered by adding white (or in the case of silk painting, diluent), black (pure black dye), or gray (diluent and black) in three ways:

- A hue plus white (diluent) produces a *tint* (a light value) of that hue.

- A hue plus black produces a *shade* (a dark value) of that hue.

- A tint plus black produces a *tone* (a muted, medium value) of that hue.

Intensity is how bright a hue looks. The outer ring of a color wheel shows hues at their most intense. To alter the intensity

This color wheel clock was painted on silk, using the 9 basic Pébéo Soie-brand mixing colors. It displays hues in the outer ring, along with shades, hues mixed with their complements, and tints in the second, third, and fourth rings respectively.

and make a color more subtle, add either a touch of its complementary color or black. The resulting less-intense hues are either *neutrals* (made by mixing equal parts of each complement) or *semi-neutrals* (three parts of one complement to one part of the other, or a variation of this ratio); these are also called *earth tones*.

COLOR WHEEL

An artist's color wheel is a worthwhile investment for this project and for future reference because it will serve as a guide for color harmonies, as well as for hues, tints, shades, and tones. You can buy a color wheel in any art supply store, or you can make one yourself on silk. For this color wheel, I used the French-made Pébéo Soie (*soie* is French for silk) dyes, which are highly concentrated and become more brilliant when diluted. I chose 9 basic mixing colors, plus black, but Pébéo offers a collection of 80 colors. The basic procedure for making the wheel is outlined here.

Stretch a piece of silk no smaller than 14 inches square on a frame. On a piece of tracing paper, draw the wheel guidelines, dividing the circle into 12 sections and 4 concentric rings. Section 12 in the circle will correspond to 12 o'clock on a watch face, section 1 falls immediately one space to the right at 1 o'clock, and so on. Place this pattern under the framed silk and apply gutta resist following the lines of your drawing, which should show through the fabric.

Next, prepare your palette. Place a small amount—no more than a teaspoon—of each of the dye colors in its own small cup and arrange them together on a tray following the order below. You are now ready to apply the dye. For the outer ring, beginning with section 12, I've listed the section and its hue—along with the Pébéo dye names in parentheses:

12. yellow (for a cooler color, use Primary Yellow 01 alone, or for a warmer color mix it with Buttercup 03)
  1. yellow-orange (Buttercup 03)
  2. warm red-orange (Red Poppy 07)
  3. cool orange-red (Pomegranate 15)
  4. red/rhodamine (Bougainvillea 12)
  5. red-violet/purple (Fuchsia 09)
  6. violet (Bougainvillea 12 and a touch of Cyan 28)
  7. blue-violet/reflex blue (Cobalt Blue 24)
  8. blue/process blue (Cyan 28)
  9. green/blue-green (Jade 33)
10. green/green-yellow (Primary Yellow 01 with a bit of either Jade 33 or Cyan 28)
11. yellow-green (also Primary Yellow 01 with a bit of either Jade 33 or Cyan 28—just in different proportions).

The second ring is comprised of shades of the hues made by mixing a small amount of black with each dye color. For the third ring, alter the intensity of the hues with the corresponding complementary colors (making semi-neutrals). And finally, in the fourth ring, place tints of each hue made by mixing the hue with diluent. Again, you will need no more than a teaspoon of each dye mixture. Now, with your color wheel in hand, you are ready to proceed.

WORKING WITH COLOR HARMONIES

As I travel and teach workshops around the country, I have noticed that many silk painters, including myself, limit themselves to a few favorite color combinations (or harmonies) that they use repeatedly in their artwork. These color harmonies have usually been developed through years of painting and are often very sophisticated, reflecting the artist's personal sense of style.

When I was involved in producing surface designs for the textile industry, stylists would ask me to develop patterns using specific sets of colors, often reflecting color trends not in my repertoire. Sometimes these color combinations would even offend my aesthetic sensibilities, but as I reached beyond the limitations of personal taste to work with these colors, my ability to mix, use, and appreciate color expanded. Thanks to this imposed discipline, I am now able to solve color and design problems for customers and clients who have specific requests and needs, as well as use color more effectively for my own artistic expression.

To expand your own color repertoire, I suggest you set aside the time to practice designing in various color harmonies, which are sometimes referred to as themes or schemes. Before you begin working on a design, it is best to choose the basic hues for the scheme, mix the colors, and store them in labelled jars. You can also premix the desired values and intensities, or create them as you paint. The color combinations you choose should be developed from the color theory and schemes outlined below. For these exercises, you may want to choose an abstract design so that you are better able to focus on color and composition without worrying about drawing. After this practice, the theory should become second nature to you, allowing your color expression to be intuitive, creative, and more versatile.

Monochromatic Color Scheme

For this exercise, choose a pure hue and develop a design by altering only its value and intensity. Works created with only varying tints, tones, and shades of one hue can be very dramatic. Keep in mind that active areas are created with strong contrasting values (lights and darks), while quiet areas use values that are more closely related. In silk painter Gay Lynette Morris's *Atlantic Natica* (opposite page) the darker values create a sense of depth and texture in the crevices of the shells, and these alternating lights and darks also add an interesting striped pattern.

The discipline of working with a monochromatic color scheme will help you understand how value and intensity are very basic and important aspects of composition. This also holds true when you are working in any of the other color schemes presented here.

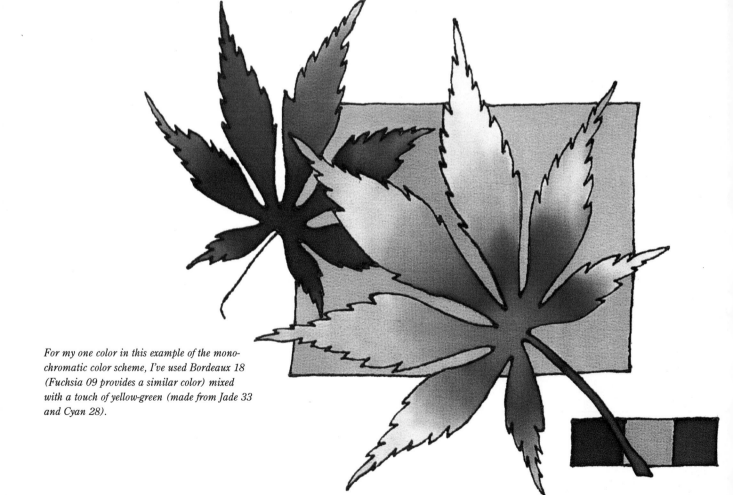

For my one color in this example of the monochromatic color scheme, I've used Bordeaux 18 (Fuchsia 09 provides a similar color) mixed with a touch of yellow-green (made from Jade 33 and Cyan 28).

ATLANTIC NATICA. © Gay Lynette Morris. *Here you see the monochromatic color scheme in use in a finished painting. The shells are all tints, tones, and shades of the same salmon-rust color.*

Complementary Color Scheme

Complementary colors are called such because, when used together, they enhance each other's value and intensity. For example, yellows are more vibrant when placed in a field of violet, and the reverse is also true. In a pair of complementary colors, one is cool and the other is warm, and when mixed together, they neutralize each other (hence the previously defined term *neutrals*). Often a successful complementary composition will include only the neutrals and very little, if any, of the pure complementary hues.

To apply this theory, choose a set of complementary colors, and premix a range of different values (tints, shades, tones) and intensities (neutrals and semi-neutrals) to work within your design. Do this exercise twice, the first time using only the neutrals and semi-neutrals (without the pure complementary hues) in your design. For your second endeavor, use the semi-neutral and neutral colors as the main colors, with the two pure complementary hues as accents. Notice how the semi-neutrals bring the pure hues to life.

These leaves illustrate the complementary color scheme of blue (Cyan 28) and orange (Buttercup 03 mixed with a touch of Red Poppy 07). Notice how the complementary hues enhance one another.

TORCH GINGER. © Gay Lynette Morris. *The exotic red flowers against the green leaves in this beautiful silk painting demonstrate a complementary color scheme. Note, too, the use of black gutta, as an integral part of the design, to outline the flower petals and leaves.*

COLORADO FARM. © Gay Lynette Morris. *Here the artist has basically developed a complementary color scheme with neutrals to work in a landscape scene. The touch of yellow-orange against a violet-blue sky are complements, while the red roofs, blue-green hills, and yellow-green trees create a split-complementary scheme.*

The complementary color scheme (orange and blue) with its neutrals is easily identifiable in these leaves.

Split-Complementary Color Scheme

A split-complementary scheme is achieved by introducing one complementary color to an analogous color scheme. The complement becomes the accent color in the split-complementary scheme, and can be used in very spontaneous and exciting ways to add creative spark to a design or composition. Pick either three or five analogous colors; the complementary color is the hue directly across the wheel from the middle color of your chosen sequence. For example, three analogous colors could be blue, blue-violet, and violet. The complementary color for this group would be yellow-orange.

A blue-violet, blue, and blue-green (Cobalt Blue 24, Cyan 28, and Jade 33 respectively) are used in this analogous color scheme.

The split-complementary color scheme shown here is comprised of blue-violet (Cobalt Blue 24 and a touch of Fuchsia 09), blue (Cyan 28), and blue-green (Jade 33) for the analogous colors, with an earth-tone orange (Buttercup 03 with a touch of Pomegranate 15 and Jet Black 80) for the complementary ones.

MOON RISING OVER PUEBLO.© Gay Lynette Morris. *This scene employs a split-complementary color scheme. The blue windows and doors against the orange earth tone of the buildings show a bold use of complements, while the blue-green and blue-violet hills in the background complete the scheme.*

Triad Color Scheme

Color triads are composed of three colors that are equidistant from each other on the color wheel. There are only four basic combinations: the primary colors —red, yellow, and blue; the secondary colors—orange, violet, and green; and two sets of tertiary colors—yellow-orange, red-violet, and blue-green, and red-orange, blue-violet, and yellow-green. Triads used in varying tints, tones, shades, and intensities make dynamic and interesting combinations. For drama and strength in a design, one color of the triad should dominate, with the other two used in unequal proportions.

The color triad in these leaves is comprised of yellow-gold (Buttercup 03 and a touch of Jet Black 80), blue-green (Jade 33 with a bit of Primary Yellow 01), and red-violet (Fuchsia 09).

JERICHO. © Gay Lynette Morris. *The predominant use of the red, yellow, and blue color triad, along with the corresponding neutrals, brings this color composition together.*

Dominant Hue Color Scheme

Using a dominant hue is another way to unify a painting. Natural light seems to harmonize our surroundings by imbuing them with a small amount of the same color. This dominant hue brings all the colors into harmony and creates a mood. For example, a landscape bathed in the light of a sunset will take on a reddish cast; on a rainy day the landscape will take on a blue-violet cast.

In silk painting, many colors are often mixed by overpainting (painting one color over another on the silk) and the use of a dominant hue will integrate the design, slightly neutralizing and reducing the intensity of any unmixed hues in the composition. Your colors will be richer, earthier, and more coordinated once you become more familiar with the dominant hue theory and apply it to your silk painting.

Here a tone of sky blue (Cyan 28 and Cobalt Blue 24 diluted and mixed with a touch of Jet Black 80) is the dominant hue placed over blends of Bougainvillea 12, Buttercup 03, sky blue (undiluted and without black), and Primary Yellow 01. It ties all the colors together and makes them a bit more subtle.

MISTY MORNING. © Len Brondum. *The dominant blue-violet hue creates a unifying atmosphere of early morning mist in the air and dampness on the forest floor.*

Russia, Scuzdal. © Natashe Foucault. *The dominant reddish hues of this roofscape create a sunset atmosphere over this chilly, Russian winter scene.*

Random Color Scheme

This kind of scheme is the most difficult to execute and control because there are no rules. It is also difficult to emulate. On occasion, a stylist would point out a random color scheme in a fashion magazine and ask me to use those colors in my collection of designs. I found it quite a creative challenge to develop compositions this way. On analyzing works in which color was used in a seemingly random way, I noticed that many such compositions were actually based on either a dominant complementary or a split-complementary scheme; some compositions even incorporated multiple color schemes. Inevitably, almost any color will work with another, given the right proportions, placement, and variety of shapes in a composition.

When working with a random color scheme, silk painters often begin a piece by painting motifs and images on a white ground. Since the colors are positioned randomly against this ground, the trick is choosing and mixing a background color that will set off all the hues while maintaining an overall balance. Grays, cool beiges, other neutrals, or black are often good solutions because they provide a quiet supporting ground and subtly set off all the random colors without matching or detracting from any of them. They can also be used in a border to frame and control a random scheme.

For an experienced designer, decisions on color and placement are made through a combination of personal taste and aesthetic intuition. Therefore, the most creative way to develop a design for a random color palette is to practice and work intuitively with your chosen premixed colors. When I find myself challenged by a color scheme (What hue should I use in the background? How should I balance the elements of this composition?), I refer to my collection of color swatches and to my experience in color theory and design for visual support. Although it is risky, working with this type of scheme satisfies a creative need and gives me the opportunity to strengthen my artistic judgments as well as learn from my design successes and failures.

Once you have expanded your knowledge of color by applying the various harmonies to several designs, you will be ready to take greater risks and use your creative intuition in developing or emulating random color schemes.

NOAH'S ARK. © Gay Lynette Morris. *The daughter of a missionary, Gay has drawn from the familiar teachings of her childhood to recreate this biblical scene with tropical patterns and motifs. This is the first in a series of Noah's Ark scenes that has been reproduced as limited edition posters. Here, the use of repeated shapes and a random color scheme adds variety and keeps the eye moving throughout the painting. The neutral, black and white border acts as a frame for the scene; it contrasts with the random color scheme, but the abstract pattern keeps it tied into the design.*

BUTTERFLY FISH.© Gay Lynette Morris. *This piece employs a random color scheme, but as you study it you can also see Gay's intentional and strong use of complementary (red against green) and split-complementary (yellow against blue-violet, violet, and red-violet) schemes within the total composition. Like most accomplished artists, she uses color both to articulate form and to provide compositional balance.*

LORIKEETS (detail). © Linda France Hartge and David Hartge. *Linda's beautiful color schemes are often seemingly random in nature, but on closer examination her strong use of complementary and split-complementary colors within the overall composition becomes apparent. Like* Butterfly Fish *(opposite page), this detail juxtaposes red against green and yellow-orange against blue-violet.*

3 BUILDING A FOUNDATION

Silk painting has the ability to satisfy our intrinsic need to develop and express ourselves as artists. This is one of its greatest beauties. People with little, if any, previous art experience are drawn to the medium and enthusiastically learn basic techniques. Then, stimulated by the seemingly endless possibilities and challenges of working with silk, they delve into more creative projects.

Technical skills are essential to the growth of an artist and to success in the undertaking of more advanced endeavors. Silk painters must make a commitment to acquire and improve their design and composition abilities. And, since the balance of skills and challenge is essential to the growth of an artist, I am always inspired when my students strive to interpret new subject matter or express new moods, rather than simply ask, "What else can I do with salt and alcohol techniques?" At this point, I can sense that they are beginning to grasp the diversity and potential of the medium and are ready to confront new goals.

WHITE RHODODENDRON. © Evelyn Jenkins Drew

DEVELOPING DESIGN IDEAS

I often recommend that the novice artist enroll in color and design, drawing, or painting courses. These basic art classes teach the meaning of line, form, space, texture, and color — the fundamental elements of design. While studying these concepts in relation to composition, the principles of art — balance, pattern and repetition, rhythm, movement, and contrast — will also be discovered. It is also in these classes that individual design ideas and preferences begin to surface.

This recommendation may seem somewhat intimidating. While silk painting is definitely an art, people who become interested in it don't necessarily think of themselves as artists or as having the ability to become artists. But experience as both a teacher and student has taught me that knowledge and mastery are learned, not inherited. Individual aptitudes for art may determine the ease or difficulty with which you develop artistic capabilities, but ultimately, motivation and discipline are the keys to artistic growth. Time spent honing basic design skills is well invested, because ability and creativity often improve with age.

Research is one of the best ways to learn and gather ideas. Fashion, interior design, and fine art magazines are a good source of many motifs and color schemes. These ideas can then be combined in a fabric design, garment, or painting in new and creative ways. As artists develop, so do their research processes. For example, you might find yourself frequenting museums or clothing boutiques; craft fairs are also educational because, like art classes, they afford the opportunity to see what other artists are doing. Eventually, you will tailor your methods of research to suit your individual needs and style. Once you have this foundation, your medium will become a less-intimidating source of inspiration.

EXPLORING DESIGN THROUGH DRAWING

When people ask me where I get my own inspiration, my first response is, "drawing." Drawing is a crucial form of artistic research and development. As you learn to draw, you learn to see and understand your environment from a different and more visual, aesthetic perspective. And, you learn how to communicate visually. Many artists speak of this process as becoming "visually literate." Just as hearing music through a musician's ear, and with a musician's knowledge, can only heighten the listening experience, the ability to see with an artist's eye can only enhance one's life and art.

As a discipline, drawing will inspire you and teach you many interesting ways to interpret subject matter. It will help you discover or better observe the textures and spatial relationships occurring in the environment. The natural patterns, rhythms, and contrasts found all around us are the very elements we need to inspire our compositions. But you are only as good as your drawing ability, because, as with any language, you can express yourself only up to your level of development, whatever it may be. Whether composing an abstract or a representational image, don't let your ideas be held at the mercy of your drawing skills; it is to your advantage to improve this craft so that you can communicate in any way and at any level you choose.

Artist Linda France Hartge's exquisitely designed and drawn silk paintings clearly illustrate the influence of nature on the artist and the importance of drawing. While doing research, she and her partner David Hartge of Kaleidosilk became interested in a species of carp known as koi. These fish are bred for form and color by the Japanese to grace their water gardens. Linda translated the textures and patterns she discovered while observing the koi in their lily ponds into her designs; and as she researched and painted them, her interest in the fish became more intense. Both Linda and David were so fascinated by their subject matter that they became active members of a club devoted to studying and breeding award winning, beautifully marked and proportioned koi. Linda pays such close attention to detail in her drawings that koi enthusiasts have recognized the champion koi, called Tancho Sanshoku, in her painting *Tancho* (on the page opposite).

CLOWN TRIGGER. © Linda France Hartge and David Hartge. *Drawing is a form of observation and of gathering information. Linda observed and was truly inspired by the fish's combinations of bold motifs and colors, which are not merely decorative but function as natural protective camouflage from predators. Her drawing and design skills enabled her to convey the patterns and rhythms found in nature.*

TANCHO. © Linda France Hartge and David Hartge. *Linda used the champion koi, Tancho Sanshoko, as a reference when composing this painting. Once she understood the fish's basic form, she eliminated some of its natural elements and enhanced others, effectively stylizing her image. For example, the ripples that surround Tancho have been stylized. Due to her familiarity with the subject through observation and drawing, Linda was still able to preserve the essence of the fish despite any artistic liberty she may have taken. For this reason, koi enthusiasts can identify Tancho and consider the painting an unofficial portrait.*

KOI GARDEN (screen). © Linda France Hartge and David Hartge. *These lines are so seductively drawn, the colors so rich, and the perspective so inviting that the viewer can't help but think he is actually standing on a footbridge overlooking this pond. To create a painting with such feeling involves a combination of drawing, composition, and silk painting skills. Linda first explored her subject (the Japanese garden pond) by sketching it. To counteract the vertical thrust of the screen frames, she devised a composition that placed images horizontally across the separate sections, ultimately creating three horizontal movements to balance the three vertical screen panels. The slightly diagonal cat-o'- nine-tails near the edges of the painting stop the horizontal flow and keep the eye within the painting. The vertical and diagonal positions of the koi also interrupt the lateral motion. The lily pads float on the pond surface and create a sense of space and depth. They also move toward the viewer, inviting him into the scene.*

BLUE HERONS RISING. © Len Brondum. *The repeated image of the cat-o'-nine-tails creates vertical lines to contrast the circular grid that flows throughout this painting. Len uses the structure of this grid, which emulates ripples in a pond, to break down her shapes, colors, and composition, creating an abstraction of the forms found in nature.*

TULIPS. © Ute Patel-Missfeldt. *In this unusual image, Ute combines both a realistic and a stylized representation of the tulip. The flowers above ground are accurately drawn, twisting and reaching for the sunlight much as they would in nature. It is below the surface that the more two-dimensional, stylized design occurs in the oval-shaped bulbs with their radiating halos of color and stiff, projecting roots. This stylization effectively highlights the difference between what is above and what is below the earth's surface. From the book* Jugendstils, *published by Eulen Verlag.*

EXPLORING ABSTRACTION

Rather than focusing on realistic depictions of objects, silk painters like Suzanne Punch explore the elements of design and principles of art purely for their own sakes. This type of expression, called abstract art, requires experience (in both figurative and abstract representation) and a willingness to aggressively explore the potential of the medium.

Suzanne pays special attention to the negative space—the background or areas between the motifs—in her floral paintings and garments. In these compositions, this negative space is always vibrant, well designed, and in balanced proportion to the positive areas (the subject matter or motif). As a result, the entire piece is more harmonious when finished. In her abstract paintings, she focuses on the spatial concerns of merging texture, color, and shape to create the illusion of deep space. This quality of joining space from different planes in a two-dimensional medium is called *plasticity*. Without this there is no sense of depth, and the forms remain forever floating on the picture (or surface) plane. To create a feeling of three dimensionality, Suzanne uses the inherent whiteness of the silk as the lightest value and creates her space relationships with multiple layers of dye and resist.

Color and light are integral tools in creating the illusion of depth and can be used in many ways. In some cases, lighter hues bring images or spaces closer to the foreground, or picture plane, of a painting. This occurs with the bright fish in artist Jacqueline Noss-Ferrero's *The Comedians* (see page 53), which swim right up to the viewer and are set off by the deeper, receding tones of the water; the dark colors of the water also lead the eye back further into the scene. The opposite is true in artist Natashe Foucault's *Winter in Weaverville* (see page 53). In this windowsill still life, reminiscent of photorealism in its representational style, the darker, interior areas of the foreground are closer to the viewer, while the lighter snowscape pulls the eye out into the distance.

For Linda and Suzanne, and all these artists, inspiration comes from pursuing a deeper understanding of the creative process and the relationship between their environment and their medium. The devoted interest of a koi enthusiast for a certain fish, or the appreciation an avid gardener has for a particular flower, is essentially the same passion for color and form. Since they have developed their technical skills as silk painters, these artists are able to express their involvement with their subject matter visually through their art.

FAST WATERS AT GIVERNY. © Suzanne Punch. *Here, resist is used to suggest the rapid movement and undercurrents of water. After creating this initial feeling of motion, the challenge for Suzanne is to suspend the areas of warm color in the midst of all that fluid coolness. Although warm colors usually convey energy and vibration, here they create islands of calm (resembling reflective patches of sunlight) that contrast the direction of the diagonal resist strokes.*

GRASSES. © Suzanne Punch. *When we view art, we subconsciously bring our previous visual history into that present moment. These past experiences provide a context within which we automatically assume and expect certain things to be true. In this painting, the strong horizontal division with blue color above, which we will always see as sky, leads us to read the vertical brushstrokes below as grass. Any surrounding elements, no matter how abstract, will also be incorporated into that interpretation.*

BRIDGE II. © Suzanne Punch. *Using a technique much like the action painting pioneered by Jackson Pollock in the 1960s, Suzanne literally flung dye and resist at the silk with no preconceived notions about composition. In doing so, she challenges herself to explore her own creative potential in relation to the behavior of the medium. She also relies on the intuitive expression of her artistic skills for color and formal solutions. In this case, the light lines of white resist provide highlights, and the central dark, arching lines become a "bridge" that serves as both a visual and psychological escape from the menacing areas of the foreground. This bridge also creates depth as it guides the eye back and forth from the larger, warm-hued shapes in the front to the receding, cool-colored shapes in the distance.*

THE COMEDIANS. © Jacqueline Noss-Ferrero. *This whimsical painting combines representational drawing with abstraction. The fish, although stylized and slightly comical, are expressive and fairly realistic. In the background, on the other hand, Jacqueline explores abstract impressions of the forms, textures, space, and light found in the ocean environment. To do this she combines salt, alcohol, and wet-on-wet techniques, which all help to emulate the feel of deep ocean water. The salt technique involves placing salt crystals on freshly painted silk. The salt pulls the wet dye in various directions, creating interesting swirls and shapes. The alcohol technique also produces unusual patterns when droplets of alcohol diluent are carefully splattered on a painted ground. In the wet-on-wet technique the silk is first dampened with alcohol diluent and then decorated with dye. In this way, the shapes of color spread slowly and dry with a softer edge.*

WINTER IN WEAVERVILLE. © Natashe Foucault. *Natashe creates a mood and multiple planes by contrasting realistic and abstract elements. The clear, cozy interior is distinctly separate from the icy, obscure landscape behind it. The warm hues and expertly drawn objects invite the viewer into a homey, familiar environment and focus attention on this foreground space, which is very close to the picture plane. By comparison, the cool colors of the hazy background pull this space even further into the distance.*

4 SURFACE DESIGN

Silk painters often use their original fabric designs to create fashions and home furnishings. Knowing and using a specific "layout," called a surface design, that is conducive to your application will help you achieve more finished, professional-looking results. Surface designs provide guidelines that help you solve specific visual and placement problems when creating a layout. Artists who understand surface design layouts create patterns that are both unique and consistent in quality, and in the process, they also cut down on fabric waste.

It is important for the silk painter to understand the design principles behind these layouts. Form should follow function, not compete with it. Just as the shape of a garment is constructed to flow with and flatter a person's figure, so should the surface design. For instance, a vertical stripe on a skirt may be more flattering than a horizontal one, which widens the figure. The same is true for home furnishings; the surface pattern should work with the object's intended use. For example, fabrics with vertical stripes are more appropriate for draperies because the direction of the motif gives an increased sense of height to the room and windows.

BLACK, WHITE, AND COLOR (detail). © Joanell Connolly.
Photo by the artist

FALLING LEAVES. © Susan L. Moyer. *This scarf employs the various motif placements described here, as illustrated in the three details shown below.*

THE THREE BASIC LAYOUTS

There are three basic ways to orient the elements, or motif, in a surface design. This placement is referred to as the layout. Elements can all be placed in the same direction, in other words with their tops and bottoms pointing the same way; or, they can be placed in different directions, meaning their tops and bottoms face different ways. In the following descriptions and the three illustrations (shown below), I use a leaf motif to indicate direction or orientation (and also lack thereof). These layouts apply to most other motifs as well. The three basic layouts are:

- *allover nondirectional* (no top or bottom): leaves are scattered all over with stems facing in all directions; the layout will work any way.

- *allover one-directional* (top and bottom): leaves are scattered all over with stems facing either up or down; the layout will work only one way.

- *two-directional* (top and bottom reversible): leaves are scattered with some stems facing up and others facing down; the layout will work two ways.

Besides being oriented in a certain direction, the motifs in a design are often carefully spaced, and this also contributes to the overall surface design layout. The basic arrangements are as follows:

- *tossed:* there is some ground, or space, between the individual elements — in this case, the leaves.

Here, the three top rows of leaves are placed in a one-directional set motif, which then changes to a two-directional set motif in the next two rows.

In the middle of this section of the scarf a one-directional tossed motif is used.

Moving toward the end of the scarf, the design incorporates a nondirectional tossed motif, which gradually becomes a nondirectional packed motif at the very bottom with only a little background visible.

Toucan and Parrot. © Susan L. Moyer. *This silk painting makes use of nondirectional and two-directional layouts. The crescents are nondirectional and the leaves and zigzag stripes are two-directional.*

- *packed:* little, if any, ground appears between the elements of the motif.
- *set:* the motif is set in rows either vertically or horizontally, or it is arranged symmetrically.

More than one type of layout can be incorporated in a design. For example, an allover nondirectional leaf motif can be tossed over a ground pattern such as a texture or stripe. In my painting

Toucan and Parrot (above), three layouts are incorporated into one surface design: the crescent shapes are placed in a tossed and nondirectional manner, the leaves are tossed in a two-directional layout, and the zigzag stripes are also two-directional. For more examples, explore the latest fashions and fabrics, and try to identify the layouts employed by a range of surface designers. As you work with the following basic design exercises, you will begin to see that infinite variations are possible.

WORKING WITH DESIGN

These exercises teach the principles behind surface design layouts and the guidelines for executing them. They utilize basic geometric shapes in a tossed layout. It may take time and practice to get to the point at which these principles become intuitive, so be patient. Perseverance will give you a foundation for an endless amount of design ideas and will enable you to creatively break the rules to produce more successful, professional-looking wearable art and home-furnishing fabrics.

Materials

18- by 24-inch tracing paper (pad or roll)

pencils

kneaded eraser

T square

right angle

scissors

clear tape

In addition, you might find these optional design aids helpful:

Bodice template. Shaped like the front of a size 8 strapless bodysuit, the template is placed over a surface design to check if the size, placement, and direction of the motif elements compliment the shape of the body.

Proportion wheel. Used by graphic designers, the proportion wheel helps you calculate the amount by which you need to reduce or enlarge a particular motif when adapting its size to the proportions of the garment or other project you're incorporating it into. It is most helpful when you are enlarging or reducing a design on a copy machine and need the actual percentage. For example, if you have a motif that is 2½ inches wide and you want to enlarge it to 4¾ inches, the proportion wheel will determine that 4¾ is 190 percent of 2½; therefore, you would enlarge a 2½ inch motif 190 percent (on the copier) to make it 4¾ inches. Likewise, the wheel would tell you that to adapt a motif that appears on a 36-inch-square scarf to the proportions of a 45-inch-square scarf, you would enlarge the motif by 125 percent.

The Exercises

Draw all the basic design shapes — circles, squares, triangles, and crescents — on a piece of tracing paper and then cut them out. You will probably need at least 20 of each shape. For each layout type, experiment with the placement of the various shapes, using another sheet of paper as your practice background surface. Move the shapes around, perhaps even overlapping them. To give yourself ample space, each practice surface should be no smaller than 18 by 22 inches. Once you are satisfied with your layouts, affix the motifs to the paper with tape. Remember to use the bodice template to check the movement of each layout.

Try all of the following:

- allover nondirectional circles in a tossed layout
- allover nondirectional squares in a tossed layout
- allover nondirectional triangles in a tossed layout
- allover nondirectional crescents or curved lines in a tossed layout
- allover nondirectional combined shapes in a tossed layout
- allover nondirectional motif with a directional motif. One example of this layout might incorporate stripes (directional motif) with tossed (nondirectional) circles.

A bodice template cut from black paper is placed over sketches of two nondirectional surface designs to see if the layout will flatter a woman's silhouette.

Snapshots were used as a drawing reference for a floral motif, and the proportion wheel was then used to determine the percentage of reduction or enlargement of the elements to be incorporated into the design and layout.

Guidelines for placement of motifs in a layout

• Keep the eye moving throughout the design. Awkward placement distracts the eye from the overall motif. On an article of clothing, this might be the unflattering effect created when a motif falls on each breast or on the backside. On a pillow, minor design elements might fall in a central area while more important details are cut off or fall to the side, disturbing the balance. To avoid these occurrences, make sure the positioning of the motifs in each layout doesn't create strong diagonals, horizontals, verticals, or symmetry (unless, of course, this is specifically intended). The bodice template helps you check these aspects.

• Work with an odd number of elements and vary the size of the motifs for added interest and movement.

• Avoid large spiky motifs, which are visually harsh. In garments, they will interrupt the body silhouette and stop eye movement.

• Add curves, such as stems and leaves, to motifs and straight objects to soften a design and give it a feeling of motion.

• Avoid placing motifs in a completely vertical or horizontal position.

• Place some of the motifs so they "bleed" off or go beyond the borders of the design.

• Keep the negative space balanced and interesting by varying the size or placement of the individual motif elements so that enough (but not too much) background space is visible.

SUNDAY TIMES 1994 (long vest). © Jane Herzenberg Design Studio. Photo by Robert Toby. Model: Emily Sunderman. *Jane Herzenberg, who has studied surface design, uses abstract, nondirectional backgrounds as a backdrop for her realistic, conversational subject matter (here a coffee cup, sugar cubes, and newspaper). Her fun, unique wearable art is constructed from beautifully designed and engineered patterns.*

UNTITLED. © Marcuse. Photo by Lindy Powers.
*Michelle Marcuse created this interesting ensemble
by contrasting similar colors with various surface
design layouts. The pants were cut from a fabric
with a two-directional stripe design, while the
blouse was spot-placed on a fabric with a diagonal
V-stripe design. The jacket was constructed from
silk with a nondirectional layout that incorporates
design motifs found in both the blouse and pants
fabrics.*

UNTITLED. © Marcuse. Photo by Lindy Powers. *This beautiful
silk charmeuse ensemble by Michelle Marcuse incorporates two basic, abstract
surface design patterns (two-directional and nondirectional) over a nondirectional
blended background. The culotte fabric bears a two-directional motif, while the full-
length duster coat displays the nondirectional pattern. Also note that the long-
sleeved blouse and coat-lining fabrics have two very different nondirectional
scattered layouts. Michelle uses the blended backgrounds and matching color
scheme to coordinate her painted fabrics.*

PAISLEY. © Tamara Maas. *Tamara is a professional silk painter who produces surface designs for the fashion industry. The fabric in this jacket is an example of one of her industrially-printed designs that was originally painted on silk. The nondirectional layout was repeated and printed on polyester yardage.*

PAISLEY (detail). © Tamara Maas

HATS. © Leo Loomie, Artisans Textiles. *Leo markets one-of-a-kind hats made from his collection of striped, handpainted silk fabrics.*

FARBRAUSCH. © Ute Patel-Missfeldt. *The bodice, collar, sleeves, and belt of this painted-silk coat were constucted out of an engineered design. To do this, the artist drew the surface design on the pattern pieces prior to painting to ensure that the images would fall in the desired places once the garment was con-structed. The fabric was then painted. From the book* Seidenmonde mit Phantasie, *published by Eulen Verlag.*

PLANNING SURFACE DESIGNS FOR FASHION

There are two main ways to approach designing fabric that is intended for wearable, rather than fine, art. The first is to spot-place the paper pattern pieces for the garment on a chosen area of previously painted fabric. This means that you let the surface design of the already-painted cloth guide your garment pattern placement. For example, you could place a skirt pattern piece so that its hemline falls along the fabric's border design. After you've decided on placement, pin the pattern pieces to the fabric, cut them out of the fabric, and sew them together following the

pattern sewing instructions. The surface design will fall in the predetermined areas.

The second method is to engineer a design. In this way, the placement of the motif is first specifically planned to move with and complement the lines of a garment, and then the fabric is painted accordingly. When laying out an engineered design, it is also important to consider how the motif will fall on the body when the item of clothing is worn. For example, a motif could be designed to flow from the bodice of a dress onto a sleeve, or from the front of a jacket onto the back. To execute an engineered design, first preshrink the unpainted silk (as explained

DRESS. © Marcuse. Photo by Lindy Powers. *The bodice of this dress is constructed from fabric with a nondirectional, set design that has been machine smocked. This is done by gathering the cloth in randomly spaced, round bunches and stitching it in place. The nondirectional striped effect on the skirt is created both by vertical handpainted stripes and horizontally positioned strips of fabric over the blue skirt. The bright, vibrating colors add depth to this already dramatic concept.*

QUILTED PEACOCK JACKET. © Linda France Hartge and David Hartge. *Another example of an engineered design, this jacket also incorporates machine embroidery and quilting (a technique covered in chapter 5). The stitching adds texture and dimension to the design. Note that Linda avoids absolute symmetry by placing the eyes of the feathers and the fuchsia threads at different heights on a background of randomly stitched lines.*

in chapter 1) before you begin so that your painted design will not shrink during the steam-setting process. Then mount it onto a frame. You may need to work on a few frames of stretched silk depending on how much fabric your garment requires.

Draw the intended motifs on your paper pattern pieces. Lay these paper pieces on your stretched, framed silk and trace their outlines onto the fabric using a washable fabric pencil (which is available at sewing stores). Remove the paper and draw the motif designs in resist on the unpainted, stretched, and framed silk. You are now ready to apply the dyes. For consistency of pattern and color, you should paint all areas of your fabric at the same time, even if they don't incorporate the motif. It is also wise to paint some extra fabric so you have some creative options; if you decide, for example, to add a matching sash to a dress, you will have the cloth to do it with. Once you have finished painting the silk and the dyes are steam-set, you can cut the pieces of fabric out (following the original garment pattern outlines that you drew in resist) and sew them together as you would when constructing any garment. Try to avoid fabrics such as crepe that stretch and lose their shape easily; otherwise your pattern pieces may not maintain their forms throughout the stretching, painting, and steaming processes.

5 FASHION AND FASHION ACCESSORY PROJECTS

When designing functional objects such as scarves, pillows, and ties, always remember the architect Louis Sullivan's guiding principle: form ever follows function. This dictum was adopted by the Bauhaus, a school of architecture and design founded in Germany in the early 1920s, whose main artistic goal was to attain a synthesis of technology, craftsmanship, and design aesthetics. Silk painters, too, must know how to plan specific projects and handle the silk so they can design and construct fashions and fashion accessories that are practical as well as beautiful. The information in this chapter is intended to provide the foundation for creating successful work.

HIBISCUS AND STAR CHART SCARF (detail). © Linda France Hartge and David Hartge

FIRE AND ICE. © Susan L. Moyer. *Wax resist was placed over both thickened and unthickened dyes to create the design on this scarf. The border, which is an integral part of the composition, was created with wax resist brushstrokes.*

SCARVES

A scarf is the perfect canvas for the silk painter and a versatile accessory for its owner. Fashions continue to evolve with the times, but scarves have long been and probably always will be luxurious yet practical accessories. Scarves make wonderful gifts. They can be romantic, chic, functional, or festive. They frame the face and create or enhance a fashion mood. Any silk weave is appropriate for a scarf and each has its own unique feel: chiffon is light and airy, charmeuse is luxurious and sensuous, crepe has a beautiful drape and a subtle sheen.

Designing a Scarf

When planning a scarf design layout, many beginning silk painters arrange the main image or motif details in the center field of the scarf and frame the composition with a wide but simple straight border. As a result, when the scarf is draped around the neck or over a shoulder, the painting becomes lost in the folds, leaving only the simple border exposed. Therefore, if you are creating a scarf that is to be used as a fashion accessory rather than a painting, it may be wiser to plan a more interesting border with a simple central field. In this way, your design will

FRINGED CAT. © Judith Bateman and Suzanne Bateman-Smith. *The border on this scarf is effectively integrated with the overall design.*

MORNING GLORY AND BAMBOO. © Linda France Hartge and David Hartge. *The bold colors in this scarf make it a striking fashion accessory.*

not be lost in fabric folds. The main field can still be full of subtle textures, colors, and patterns that will echo the border design and compliment and frame the face, but the more visible border should be the most intricate area. Be creative. When planning a border, keep in mind the shape of your scarf. What design elements should fall on the corners of a square scarf and on the ends of an oblong or rectangular scarf? Rather than repeating the same images and colors on each corner, paint these areas to complement each other. As silk painter Linda France Hartge points out, "Scarves often have distinctive images in each corner, often with a narrative relationship between them."

Rolled Scarf Hems

The hemmed edges of scarves are traditionally hand-rolled; the end of the fabric is rolled in once or twice and then lightly slip-stitched in place by hand. A slip stitch is one in which the thread picks up only a few fibers of the fabric to hold the hem in place; in this way, the stitches are hardly visible on the right side of the garment. The rolled edge of a scarf should have an even roundness and should not be ironed flat. Unfortunately, steam-setting the dyes and ironing out wax resist, techniques that are often part of the silk-painting process, will flatten this hem. Therefore, the only way to truly maintain the round shape is to hem the scarf only after all silk-painting and dye-setting processes are complete.

However, to conserve time, I work on scarf blanks, which are prehemmed silk scarves available in some fabric and sewing supply stores and catalogues. Even though the hems may be flattened while steaming and ironing, they are often restored to a rounder shape in the final steps of the finishing process (the washing and dry cleaning). Whenever dry cleaning, I request that the rolled hem not be pressed.

SCARF. © 1993 Marcuse. Photo by Joe Mikvliak. *This surface design combines a variety of abstract motifs in an overall pattern.*

SCARF. © 1993 Marcuse. Photo by Joe Mikvliak. *This scarf is another example of the effective use of multiple abstract motifs in one composition.*

FLORAL SCARF. © Nan Hibma-Doremus. *The vibrant flowers and spontaneous wax resist brushwork keep the eye moving throughout this design.*

SCARF WITH BUCK AND PHEASANTS. © Antoinette von Grone. *The plain border on this scarf frames and sets off the central composition.*

APPLE VEST JACKET. © Linda France Hartge and David Hartge. *The layout of this garment was carefully engineered so that the apple motif would fall in a predetermined area, in this case the center of the back, making it a main design element.*

PILLOWS

Pillows, like scarves, can be earthy or elegant, whimsical or classical, the main event or a simple accent. With the proper choice of fabric and careful thought given to design, a painted-silk pillow can add a perfect decorative touch to almost any room.

Choosing the fabric is the first step. Again, keep in mind that form follows function. Will the pillow actually be used, or will it be purely decorative? Hence, which fabric weight is more appropriate? It has been my experience that pillow covers made from medium- to heavyweight silks (12mm and up) have more body, are more durable, and are easier to construct because the silk is more manageable, being less flimsy. The result is a sturdier, more professional-looking pillow. Lighter silks (5mm to 10mm) are not as opaque and must be backed with a white fabric, because when the pillow is stuffed, the filling tends to show through the silk and create distracting shadows on the painted design.

Pillows can be almost any size or shape imaginable, but the most common is the knife-edge pillow. This is a square, rectangular, or circular pillow on which the front and back panel edges are joined with a simple seam; when stuffed, it is thickest in the center and tapers off to the side seams, which have no depth. It can be either plain-front or quilted, which adds a further design element discussed below. Another pillow style is the bolster, which is oblong and usually cylindrical in shape. For the projects and suggestions in this section, I have mostly worked with the knife-edge pillow style.

Guidelines for Basic Pillow Design

Whether quilted or not, the most successful pillow compositions are those that keep the eye moving around and focused on the most visible area of the pillow. You should plan the layout carefully to ensure that the main design elements, whether abstract or representational, fall in the center of the pillow; otherwise your motif may fall on the side or slope of the stuffed pillow form or be cut off altogether, resulting in an amateurish-looking end product. This is a frequent problem for beginning designers working on knife-edge pillows, because they aren't aware of how the slope of the stuffed pillow will affect their designs. A border is therefore a handy device, for it not only serves to highlight the composition but can act as a guideline to help you keep your eye on the composition and your motif in a good, central position. If you are planning a design without a border, as in my pillow *Mountain Peony* (page 72), you should again pay especially close attention to placement so that you don't lose elements when your pillow is sewn together. The key is just to remember that when the pillow is stuffed, the resulting slope may alter your design.

QUILTED PILLOWS

Quilting on a pillow cover adds extra visual and tactile dimensions to the design. The resist lines (whether white, black, or colored) left in a silk painting after completion create a natural guideline to follow when stitching, and the underlying padding gives form to the motifs. Be sure to choose a resist that will be removed from the silk prior to quilting, because any resist that remains in the fabric will gum up your sewing machine and needle. So, metallic gutta or pigmented resists would not be appropriate for quilted projects, and all other resists, such as gutta and wax, must be completely extracted.

When choosing a fabric, opt for a plain silk weave like a habutai or broadcloth rather than a stretchy crepe, which tends to pucker and gather when it is machine quilted.

Preparing the Silk for Quilting

It is very important to preshrink all fabrics that are used to construct a quilted pillow cover, with the exception of polyester batting (discussed in the following section), which will not shrink. Preshrinking helps ensure that once sewn together, the fabrics will not pucker due to uneven shrinkage during future washing or dry cleaning. This includes any fusible interfacing (a fabric backing described below) and silk pieces used for testing and practicing. Remember that the silk on which your design is painted will already have shrunk during the dye-setting process.

To preshrink interfacing, submerge it in warm water and allow to drip dry; do not twist it to wring out the excess water. Or, you can use a steam iron on the wool/steam setting. For this method you will also need a press cloth, which is a piece of lightweight, natural-fiber fabric. On an ironing board, place the interfacing glue-side down over the press cloth. The cloth will protect the ironing board surface from any interfacing adhesive, and it will also absorb the moisture from the steaming. Hold the iron 2 inches above the inferfacing, letting the steam penetrate it for 3 to 4 seconds until it visibly stops shrinking.

Even though your painted silk will not need preshrinking at this point, it may need to be ironed before quilting to remove any wrinkles. To do this, cover the silk with a press cloth to protect it and iron, using the silk setting.

Construction

Quilted pillows get their three-dimensional look from batting, which is a fluffy, polyester material stitched onto the back of the painted silk. It is sold in sewing supply and fabric stores and is

PILLOW. © Linda France Hartge and David Hartge. *To frame and enhance the images, borders were created with strips of colored fabric.*

MALE AND FEMALE PILLOWS. © Kathy Ciocci and Alexis Ka. *This whimsical duo is set off by borders that are painted as part of the design. The borders hold the eye within the composition, and the colors provide bright accents for home decor.*

available in low-loft (thin) or high-loft (thick) varieties. When machine quilting, use a thin polyester batting, because it provides a subtle three-dimensional effect and is easier to work with. The thicker type tends to bunch up more during sewing, and the high loft distorts the design and shape of the pillow. To use, lay your silk fabric over the batting, tack the two layers together with large basting stitches (straight, holding stitches that will be removed afterward), and then apply the machine quilting stitches following your design's resist lines.

When quilting with a slippery fabric such as silk, you may find that it often slips around on the sewing machine. To combat this problem, you can stabilize the silk first as professional upholsterers do by backing it with a lightweight fusible interfacing. This is a nonwoven, synthetic fabric (also known simply as *fusible*), that has an adhesive on one side so you can attach it easily to the back of your silk according to the manufacturer's instructions. It provides the friction necessary to prevent the silk from shifting and sliding around on the batting. There are many, including Sheer Weight Fusible Pellon 906F, Lightweight Easy-Shaper, and SoSheer, and they are available in most sewing supply stores. Choose a fusible interfacing with care directions that are compatible with those of your silk, and keep in mind that they are *not* effective when used with a lightweight silk, because the adhesive may seep through to the front side of your design, ruining the painting.

Even though it is optional, I strongly recommend using an interfacing, whether it is a lightweight fusible or simply a piece of white cotton that you have basted to the back of your silk. It makes the stitching process much easier and provides an opaque backing for paintings executed on sheerer silks, which may allow the batting to show through the design. It is also most advisable to test a few brands to see which works best with your fabric.

To prepare fusible interfacing for adhering to the silk, follow these basic steps, and do a test piece first:

1. Place the interfacing glue-side down on the back side of your silk.

2. For placement, lightly fuse the silk to the interfacing by slightly pressing the two fabrics together, starting from the center of your piece and working toward the outside edge.

Now you are ready to secure the two layers together permanently. Use the transparent pressing sheet that comes with the fusible interfacing, and be sure to follow the manufacturer's directions to the letter. If there are crinkles or bubbles in your test piece and you are sure you are following the directions correctly, try a different interfacing. Also note that the fusible will add body to the silk, but the fabric should remain soft and pliable so that it does not pucker and crinkle when quilted. Remember that all interfacing material must be preshrunk.

After you have bonded the fusible to your silk, you are ready to attach the batting with quilting stitches. It is easiest to stitch along the resist lines in your design. This process is referred to as free-motion quilting, because rather than quilting in straight lines, you are moving the fabric freely in any direction to follow

MOUNTAIN PEONY. © Susan L. Moyer and Venera Hoerrmann. *The quilting on this pillow was done by hand because the design was executed with black gutta, which cannot be machine quilted.*

SHELL PILLOW. © Susan L. Moyer. *An interesting and integrated design effect is created on this machine-quilted pillow by letting the center image overlap with the border.*

the shapes in your composition. For this method, use a special open-toed embroidery presser foot. Like a regular sewing machine presser foot, the open-toed foot holds the fabric down and in position while you are stitching. But, because there is no bar between the toes, it doesn't block your view of the stitching and will allow you to see and follow your resist lines better.

To turn and move the fabric easily while stitching, discharge (remove or drop) the feed dog. The feed dog is the ridged gear below the presser foot that helps move the fabric forward through the machine as you stitch. You usually place your fabric over this and under the foot and machine needle. The feed dog rotates, and as it turns, the friction from the ridges pushes the fabric straight ahead under the needle. In free-motion quilting, it is better to remove or lower the feed dog to facilitate moving the fabric in other directions. If this is not possible, cut a piece of heavyweight paper approximately 2 by 3½ inches and tape it down over the feed dog.

After you have finished applying the quilting stitches, sew the back of the pillow to the front as you would with a plain pillow, leaving a section of one side unsewn to allow for stuffing. After inserting the filling, close the seam with a simple slip stitch.

Needles and Thread

When sewing with silk, use a new, sharp needle designed specifically for woven fabrics or a universal ballpoint needle designed for both wovens and knits. Sizes 9 to 11 U.S. (65 to 75 European) are your best choices. Test the needle by stitching a practice piece of silk (complete with interfacing) over some batting. The needle should not snag the fabric; otherwise it will destroy your project. If the needle is creating pulls, switch to a new one or try a needle with a finer point. Purchase extra needles and remember to change them often. In general, it is best to use a new needle for each project.

Purchase quality thread that is compatible with your silk color and design and that fits in the eye of the needle. The color of the

thread should also coordinate with your gutta line. You can use pure silk thread or a less-expensive, fine polyester type. Experienced sewers often use Coats & Clark Dual Duty Plus Extra Fine, Guterman, or Metrosene polyester thread. Another common choice is a polyester core, cotton-wrapped thread, which is a polyester-fiber thread covered with cotton.

If the thread breaks and frays during stitching, this may be a indication that your needle is too small for the thread. Switch to larger needle. On the other hand, if the needle is too big for the thread, the tension of the stitches will be uneven, resulting in a sloppy stitch line. In this case, switch to a smaller needle. Again make a few tests first to ensure the best results.

Pillow Stuffing

As mentioned before, once stuffed, the pillow will have shape, and this often affects the composition, which was painted when the silk was still flat. As you become more experienced, you will be better able to anticipate the pillow shape and adjust your designs as you are creating them. Pillows can be stuffed with either a loose synthetic-fiber filling or a preshaped pillow form, which is more manageable. When using loose filling, make sure you pack it evenly inside the slipcover so that the pillow is not lumpy. If using a pillow form, choose one that measures at least 1 to 2 inches larger than the actual cover so that the pillow is ful and firm. This is especially advisable with quilted pillows because a firmly and fully stuffed pillow will stretch the cover and show off the raised quilting.

A Note on Cleaning

Decorative silk pillow covers should be removed from the pillow form for washing or dry cleaning. To make this an easy task, zip pers, snaps, or Velcro closures can be constructed into the back of the pillow cover on the seam along one side or in the center o the back fabric panel. Instructions for this are included in pillow patterns.

MACHINE APPLIQUÉS

Appliqués are pieces of fabric cut out and sewn onto garments, fashion accessories, pillow covers, wall-hangings, quilts, and any other fabric background surfaces. They can be preplanned (as with an engineered design) and painted to incorporate specific creative and visually interesting abstract and representational design elements into a project. Pieces of your painted silk, which might even be odds and ends left over from previous creations, can also be successfully spot placed and appliquéd onto silks and other natural fabrics to add a creative spark to any project.

Appliqués can be a practical way to create unique fashions for children as well as adults. When designing garments for children, it is important to consider the wear and tear that their clothes undergo, and appliqués prove quite useful in this respect, as well. While you may not want to create an entire elaborate silk outfit for a potentially messy child, adding just a few handpainted silk appliqués to a premade garment of more durable fabric is an efficient method of embellishment.

As with engineering a surface design for a garment, you can plan the appliqué design and placement on paper pattern pieces. This is the most successful way to incorporate appliqués into a project because you will have accounted for them from the beginning of the design process. As with any engineered design, appliqué elements on garments should be placed in slightly asymmetrical layouts; the results will be more interesting and professional-looking. Appliqués also provide an opportunity to work with various fabric textures; for example, silk appliquéd over linen can create a very rich look.

The appliqué tips that follow are pieces of information I have gleaned from my experiences teaching some expert stylists, surface designers, pattern makers, seamstresses, and experienced home sewers in my advanced silk painting classes.

Choosing and Stabilizing Appliqué Fabric

The silks you choose for appliqués should be opaque enough so that if you sew light-colored appliqué pieces onto a darker ground fabric, the underlying color won't show through when they are stitched together. Also, the silk used for appliqués on garments should not be so thick that it disrupts the flow of the main fabric.

Silk appliqué pieces need to be stabilized so they retain their shape and are easier to handle while being stitched on. A stabilizing material akin to fusible interfacing is attached to the back of the silk to be used for appliqués prior to cutting out the actual appliqué shapes. This stabilizer has a light adhesive on both sides and is often referred to as a paper-backed fusible web. This adhesive enables you to tack down your appliqué pieces so that they don't shift around before you secure them with stitching.

There are several stabilizing products on the market. They vary in stiffness and involve various methods of application, so you will need to experiment to find the appropriate brand for your fabrics and then follow the accompanying instructions carefully. Two paper-backed fusible stabilizers that work well with silks are Wonder-Under and HeatnBond Lite. I use Wonder-Under because it has less adhesive than the others and has a somewhat softer, more flexible quality. However, even though

SEATTLE EXPERIENCE. © Susan L. Moyer. Pillow construction by Debra Jeanne Reddig, DeGray Designs. *I used the Japanese roketsu-zome wax resist technique (discussed further in chapter 7) to execute this design. After applying Wonder-Under stabilizer to the back of the silk, I then cut the design out of the fabric and used it as an appliqué. For the pillow, Debra chose textured silk fabrics that would coordinate with the colors found in the shell.*

SARAH'S LILY. © Susan L. Moyer. *This floral appliqué is made from one of many demonstration pieces that I have executed for my workshops. The overalls, which were a premade garment purchased at a craft shop, were washed and ironed before the silk appliqué was sewn to the garment. After applying Wonder-Under, I carefully cut out the design for the bib.*

this paper-backed stabilizer is easy to handle, I strongly suggest that you test its compatibility with your silks and practice your fusing techniques. They are not appropriate for sheer silks, because the adhesive will seep through the appliqué fabric, ruining your work. For sheerer silks, experiment with water-soluble embroidery facings or stabilizers such as Aqua-Solv or Sulky Solvy.

To use the paper-backed fusible web, follow these basic guidelines:

1. Preshrink the ground (main garment) fabric. If you suspect the dyes on it will bleed when the fabric is washed, prewash the item and rinse it until the rinse water runs clear.

2. Following the manufacturer's instructions, with an iron fuse the stabilizer to the wrong side of the fabric from which your appliqués will be cut. Test your iron setting. If the adhesive seeps through to the front of your appliqué fabric and causes it to become stiff, the iron is too hot.

3. After the stabilizer is successfully fused onto the fabric, cut out your appliqué designs.

4. Peel off the paper on the backside of the stabilizer to expose the adhesive.

5. Place a press cloth over the appliqués to protect them and the iron. Then carefully fuse the stabilizer to the ground fabric with the iron. (In this instance, sheer silk organza makes an excellent press cloth because you can see your work through it.) Since this is only the stabilizer and you will ultimately be securing the appliqués with a satin stitch, the iron needs only to be hot enough to lightly fuse the appliqués to the ground fabric and secure their edges.

Stitching

Once the appliqué shapes are tacked down with the stabilizer's adhesive, they must be permanently sewn down. There are several types of stitches you can use, the most versatile and useful one being the satin stitch, in which the thread is sewn back and forth over a fabric edge. The stitch can be adjusted to either cover the edge completely (resulting in a smooth, satiny ridge) or to lie flat without a ridge. It easily echoes or follows an outline left by a linear resist, while creating an additional design element, and it covers and therefore finishes the cut edge of the appliqué pieces as it attaches them to the ground fabric.

To execute a satin stitch, your sewing machine must have a variable zigzag-stitch feature. It allows you to choose the stitch width and length that will work best with your design and your fabrics, and most contemporary machines have it. The satin stitch is a tight, more closed version of the zigzag stitch. To switch the machine from a zigzag stitch mode to the satin stitch, shorten the length of your stitches. The width of the satin stitch, in relation to that of any resist lines, is an important consideration. If you are stitching over the resist lines, the widths of the stitches and the lines should match so that the thread covers the line. Otherwise, your stitches will look sloppy. Note, too, that any stitching on finer fabrics will lie flatter and look better with a narrow satin stitch of about $1/16$ to $1/8$ inch, while heavier fabrics with more body and texture can support a slightly wider stitch.

Needle size and thread are major considerations when executing a satin stitch. Try a size 9 U.S. (65 European) or 10 U.S. (70 European) universal needle and a fine machine embroidery thread. Test your needle, thread, and fabric combination and practice your stitching before starting. You should also use an open-toed presser foot, preferably one that has a wide, flanged channel on the bottom. The channel allows the raised satin stitch to pass under the foot without getting caught, and the flanged (slightly curved) edges of the channel provide flexibility in turning so you can maneuver around tight curves. Keep in mind that the stitches should interlock on the underside of the fabric so that the bobbin thread does not show on the top of the appliqué.

Frequently, when you are satin stitching your appliqués, you may need to change directions. The best advice I can give for handling this is to stop the machine and pivot the silk. Leave the needle in the fabric, raise the foot, and turn the fabric; once you have positioned the fabric as you need it, put the foot down and continue sewing. For outside curves, stop the needle as it enters the garment fabric, and then pivot. For inside curves, stop when the needle enters the appliqué fabric and then pivot. If your stitches slant at awkward or uneven angles and become difficult to control, you are not pivoting enough. If your shapes have sharp corners, you can either overlap the stitches or butt them up against each other. Either way, pivot when the needle is in the *garment,* not the appliqué. For soft curves you will not need to pivot. Just carefully follow the form. Practice your satin stitch until you understand when to pivot so as to avoid unsightly gaps on your actual project.

In order to satin stitch a silk appliqué to another fabric, you may need to use a background stabilizer to prevent tunneling (ridges that occur when stitches are sewn too tightly), pucker-ing, and shifting. The stabilizer is placed underneath the background fabric, to which it becomes attached as you sew on the appliqués; later it is simply torn away. A background stabilizer can be a sheet of tissue paper or a slightly heavier paper like newsprint; other options include ordinary plastic freezer paper or Tear-Away Soft, which work well on fine, silky background fabrics. Press And Tear and Sulky's Totally Stable are good for stabilizing knits and sweatshirt fleece, which also tend to move around on the sewing machine.

Thread Color

In general, the color of the thread should match that of the appliqué fabric. If you are sewing along resist lines, choose a thread that blends well with the color of those lines. Another very effective design option is to coordinate the appliqué thread with the garment fabric color. The matching thread visually integrates the background with the appliqués. A thread color that contrasts with both the ground and the appliqué will become a strong design element, but may detract from the appearance of the appliqué itself. A dark thread stitched over a light ground or vice-versa is still another alternative, but it may look messy, especially if your stitching isn't perfect. A thread that only coordinates with the background fabric, and not the appliqués, is something else to consider, but it will make the appliqué shapes seem smaller. You can even switch thread colors for different areas of a design. As you experiment with appliqué stitching, you will eventually discover which effects work the best in your projects.

SILK APPLIQUÉ JACKET (details). © 1995 Susan K. Tenebruso. *Susan created the pattern for this jacket and she designed her appliqués specifically to compliment the lines of the garment. She chose a beautiful, textured natural silk fabric for the jacket.*

SILK APPLIQUÉ JACKET (appliqué detail). © 1995 Susan K. Tenebruso. *Since the width of the satin stitch matches that of the narrow resist lines and the thread color blends in with the jacket and appliqué fabrics, the stitching does not detract from the subtle and delicate design.*

HANDPAINTED SILK TIES. *These ties utilize nondirectional and two-directional designs. The tie at left was created by Susan L. Moyer, the second from left and the last by Christine Mariotti, the center one by Nan Hibma-Doremus, and the rest by Joanell Connolly.. (All designs © the artists.)*

NECKTIES

During the late 1960s and early '70s, I designed and painted men's neckwear. It started with a few ties I painted for my husband, Dale. They became popular among the people he worked with, and I began to take orders. It was my first adventure into the world of business, and I found myself learning the ropes in the New York garment district. By the time this enterprise was in full swing I was filling orders for various boutiques, Saks Fifth Avenue, Neiman Marcus, Paul Stuart, and Barney's, which had just opened its doors.

I learned about proper tie construction from the highly skilled seamstresses at the Countess Mara tie company, and I picked up tips about styling from working with various neckwear buyers and the editors of the menswear magazine of the *New York Times*. The information in this section reflects the most important things I learned from these sources about designing and constructing ties. You should purchase a tie pattern (available at most sewing stores) and familiarize yourself with the included step-by-step construction processes before embarking on a tie project. My guidelines will then serve as helpful hints. If you are planning to have your ties professionally constructed in a factory, request a tie template so that you can determine the placement of your designs, especially if they are to be spot-placed.

TIES. © Louise Blumberg Designs. *The unusual stripes in these fabrics create an interesting variation on the traditional diagonal-stripe tie surface design layout. The resist line is a strong element as well.*

Tie Fabrics and Other Materials

A tie should feel soft but still have enough body to retain its shape. The silk should be at least 14mm and preferably a plain, jacquard, or twill weave. (Twill weaves are distinguished by the pattern of diagonal lines created by the individual fabric threads.) If the fabric is too lightweight it will sag and pucker, and create a wimpy knot and flimsy, curly edge. Tie fabric is cut on the bias, which means it is cut on a diagonal line that is usually at a 45-degree angle to the selvage (the edge of the fabric). Cutting on the bias makes the fabric stretchier because you are cutting diagonally across the grain (the direction of the fabric threads),

TIE BACK. © Louise Blumberg Designs. *At left is the back of a professionally constructed tie. You can clearly see both the loop (with the narrow end of the tie threaded through it) and bar tack (black stitching near the end of the center seam). Here, the loop was made from a piece of ribbon that was color-coordinated to match the tie fabric. The straight-grain fabric of the lining gives the bias-cut tie fabric shape and a finished look.*

TIE. © 1991 Marcuse. *This two-directional layout makes use of bold color combinations.*

creating more give in the cloth; it therefore falls differently than regularly cut fabric, resulting in a smoother fit and a more flowing line in most garments. A tie that is cut on the bias will lie properly, hanging flat against the body without twisting. If it twists, it was not cut on the true bias (an exact 45-degree angle).

Ties also require interfacing to help maintain their shape. There are two types commonly used in tie construction, both of them relatively lightweight but with high loft (fullness and height). One is a wool or wool/rayon blend and is dry-cleanable; the other is a synthetic. Experts at your local sewing store can help you decide which type is more appropriate for your tie. A lining fabric (usually an opaque silk or silky synthetic) covers the interfacing for a finished look.

Construction

Tie fabric is first painted, then cut, and finally, sewn together. Although there are preconstructed, unpainted tie blanks avail-

able in some craft stores, I strongly advise that you do not use them with the processes presented in this book. Silk fabric preshrinks naturally during the dyeing and setting processes, and since the premade ties are not dyed and steamed, they are not preshrunk. As a result, they become misshapen as they shrink during painting and setting, and ultimately do not lie flat and straight against the body. It is best to paint your own fabric and then construct the tie yourself.

Seams

The main seam on a tie is the center back seam. While hand slip-stitching this, you may have trouble controlling the bias-cut fabric, due to its increased stretchiness. It might help you to cut two forms out of cardboard in the shapes of each end of the tie. Place the fabric around the forms, and use them to hold the shape of the tie while applying the stitching. Remove them only after pressing the seam (see the section below).

Pressing the Tie

Traditionally the edges of a tie, where the fabric folds from the front to the back, are softly curved (or rolled) and should not be pressed flat into a sharp crease. For the well-dressed man, a flat tie is considered a fashion gaffe. So when ironing a tie, place a lightweight, natural-fiber press cloth over it, and hold the steam iron a few inches above. Allow the steam to penetrate through the press cloth for a few seconds without touching the iron to the fabric. Only the v-shaped ends of the tie should be ironed flat.

Loops and Bar Tacks

Another indication of good tie construction and design is the appearance of a fabric loop on the back of the wide end of the tie. This loop holds the narrow end in place while the tie is being worn. You can construct it out of the tie fabric or it can be a piece of ribbon in a coordinating color. The loop is usually placed 6 inches or more above the point and should be as wide as the narrow end plus ⅜ inch. Turn the ends of the loop under ¼ inch and slip-stitch it in place.

And finally, a tie is not complete without bar tacks on the backside of both the wide and narrow ends. The bar tacks are a few handsewn stitches that reinforce the ends of the center seam during the strain of tying and untying the knot.

Design Layouts for Neckties

There are two types of pattern layouts used for cutting tie fabrics. One is a spot-placed method of design in which the motifs are created expressly for the finished shape of the tie. When designing for spot-placed ties, plan for seam allowances, width of tie, and the general placement of the knot versus the design so that your images fall in the intended areas. Note that when worn, a tie should be knotted so the point reaches to the top of the pants waistband.

The more common pattern layout is for ties that are to be cut from fabrics with an allover design that is not necessarily planned specifically for ties. Since all ties are cut on the bias, directional designs like stripes will become diagonal. When painting fabric that will possibly be used for a tie, follow the guidelines for surface design layouts in chapter 4. It might help to make a tie template to check the proposed arrangement of the designs prior to cutting any fabric. Use cardboard or heavyweight paper for the template, and cut the opening to the planned width and length of your knotted tie. When using, remember to place it on top of your silk on the bias, since this is how the fabric will eventually be cut.

EDGE FINISHES

The edges of a fabric, especially those remaining exposed or in view, are important details on any garment or accessory. The Swiss-edge hem, the scarf-edge hem, and lettuce-edge hem are a few easy yet decorative techniques for finishing the edges. These hems are all variations on the adjustable zigzag stitch, so you will need this feature on your sewing machine. You will also need to plan for a ½-inch hem allowance when first cutting your silk. This allowance of fabric is necessary to ensure that your fabric does not tunnel or get jammed in the feed dog. If you did not plan for a seam allowance and are using either the Swiss-edge hem or the scarf-edge hem, you can experiment with substituting tear-away background stabilizers (used with appliqués) for this fabric

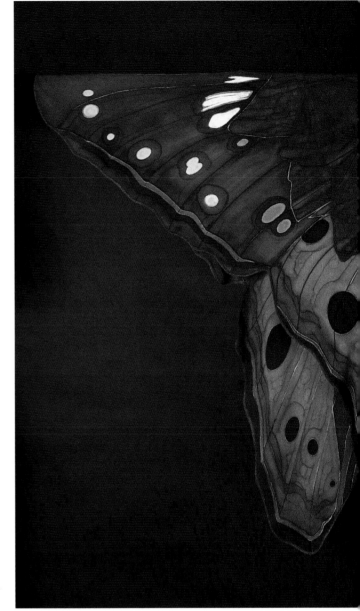

allowance. Place it under the edge of your garment where the allowance would have been and follow the directions below, treating it as you would extra fabric. Note that this technique will work when using a lettuce-edge hem; just stretch the fabric over the stabilizer to achieve the lettuce effect.

Swiss-Edge Hem

This hem edge has a round look to it due to the satin stitching over cord. It is often used as a hem for chiffon dresses.

1. Adjust your machine for 12 to 15 stitches per inch.
2. Sew a regular straight stitch where you want the edge to be.
3. Choose a color-coordinated heavyweight buttonhole twist (a thread used to finish buttonhole edges) or pearl cotton thread and place it over the stitch line.
4. Using the zigzag stitch, stitch over the cording and straight-stitch line.
5. Carefully trim off the seam allowance fabric.
6. With a slightly wider zigzag stitch, sew over this first stitching to finish the edge.

SATYRIDE. ©1994 Judy Barnes Baker. *The delicate veins on this unusual butterfly-wing cape were created by applying alcohol diluent to a dry, painted ground. The diluent lifted and pushed the dye, forming lines of more concentrated color. The edges of the wings were sealed and finished with thinned acrylic medium.*

Scarf-Edge Hem

The scarf-edge hem is comprised of a flat satin stitch. To avoid stretching the fabric, which will cause a rippled edge, firmly push the fabric toward the foot with one hand and guide it out with the other. Practice this first until you can maintain an even speed and are pleased with the results.

1. Sew a straight stitch where you want the edge to be.
2. Next, carefully turn the seam allowance under on that stitch line.
3. With the wrong side up, zigzag or satin stitch over the folded edge.
4. Carefully trim away the extra seam allowance fabric.

Lettuce-Edge Hem

Lettuce edging gets its name from its rippled, curly appearance, which sometimes resembles the edge of a lettuce leaf. It adds a decorative, frilly effect and airy movement to chiffon and other lightweight silks. This edging works the best on stretchy fabric, and especially on fabric cut on the bias. The ruffled effect is achieved by taking advantage of the fabric's stretchiness. To execute, follow the directions for the scarf-edge hem, but hold the fabric firmly with both hands and stretch it as you zigzag or satin-stitch along the edge.

Acrylic Sealers

When I was in college, I worked as an assistant to the set and costume designer of a summer theater company. We kept the uneven and unhemmed edges of some of our dance costumes from fraying by applying a thinned acrylic/polymer medium to them. To use, apply the medium to the fabric edge with a brush, let it dry thoroughly, and cut through it with sharp scissors to achieve a smooth edge. The edge of the fabric will become slightly darker and stiffer, but it will hold up through rough treatment and multiple dry cleanings and washings. As this sealed edge is somewhat less visually appealing than a stitched one, you may only want to try this method with a colored acrylic-based fabric paint like Deka. For a clear seal that makes the fabric edge look slightly darker (as if wet), use the Deka paint medium.

PART TWO: Advanced Silk Painting Techniques

Now that you are familiar with the basic silk painting concepts, you are ready for greater creative challenges. The techniques in the following chapters provide the means to execute more elaborate, complex designs. They combine methods both from other countries and other mediums, and they reveal just how versatile silk painting can be. After you have learned these more advanced approaches, you will be able to express yourself artistically without limitations.

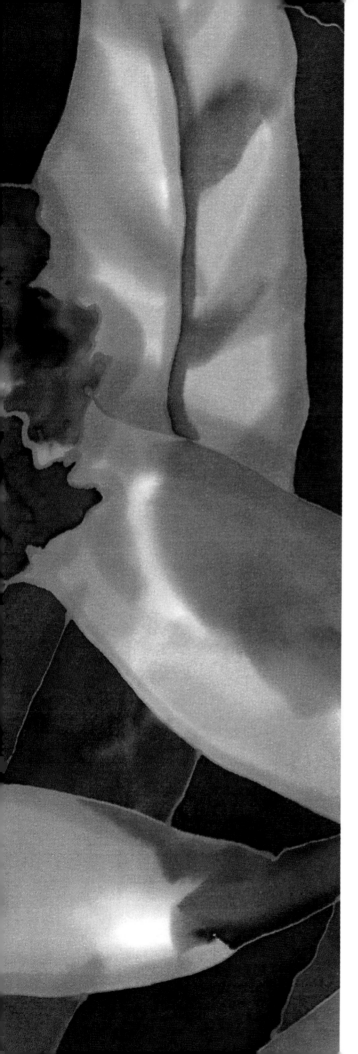

6 LINEAR UNDERPAINTING AND LAYERING TECHNIQUES

For silk painters working in their two-dimensional medium, it is natural to create and layer forms using clearly defined, highly noticeable resist lines. Any shapes are then filled in with color or shading of some sort. There may come a time, however, when you want an alternative technique, one that results in a less linear and more painterly feel. In other words, you may not want such sharp separations between elements in your design, or such obvious outlines. It is at this point that you are ready for linear underpainting.

ORCHID SPORT (detail). © Suzanne Punch

THE LIMITATIONS OF LINEAR RESISTS

Many silk painters who are accustomed to working with other, more traditional painting mediums such as oil and watercolor find that resists applied in a linear manner often restrict their ability to integrate shapes into one another or into the overall composition. This is because the linear function of resist does not lend itself well to blending and shading techniques, and the resulting line cannot be camouflaged. So the resist line not only controls the flow of the dye but becomes a strong (and not always desirable) design element in its own right as well.

In an attempt to make their silk designs more painterly, some artists experiment with tinted resists that they color-coordinate with the dyes in their paintings. However, they soon discover that using a colored resist, which would at first appear to be an ideal solution, does not really solve their problems; the introduction of another color into a painting can sometimes be even more distracting and less integrated than the use of either black or clear linear resists, because this new hue becomes another strong design element.

The Solution: Linear Underpainting

You can resolve this problem by establishing form in your design first with a linear underpainting, which you execute on the silk with dyes of varying color and intensity. This brushwork is then covered (and therefore saved) with clear gutta applied as a linear resist; in this way, the linear underpainting becomes the resist

lines. Due to their colors, which are coordinated with the dyes in the painting, these lines blend with the overall design more successfully than black, clear, or colored resist lines.

Using this technique, you can create a more painterly foundation of many hues from which you can then define and build the forms of your design. The lines become more integrated into the colors and shading of the motifs. Artist Suzanne Punch has eliminated the colored resist lines in her scarves and floral paintings by applying neutral-colored dyes as her linear underpaintings. Once she has applied the resist over those lines, she uses alcohol washes and dyes to obliterate or further soften any unwanted edges of the linear underpainting.

In the demonstration that follows, a linear underpainting serves as a versatile and painterly foundation for defining the form of the images. With this technique, the resist lines begin as simple brushstrokes of color, which are then saved with the overlay of gutta. In this way, the images are freed from being trapped in a hard-edged white, black, or colored resist outline.

Overpainting to Create Form and Depth

Oftentimes, you will want to achieve a true feel of three-dimensional space in your designs. The technique of layering images by overpainting (placing one color on top of another previously applied dye) is also shown in the demonstration. This method creates space and depth in a painting because the darker, overpainted forms recede into the background, pushing the brighter

TOUCANS. © Suzanne Punch. *The linear underpainting on this scarf is used as a strong design element. Its bold color achieves a more decorative approach, in keeping with the spirit of the design.*

areas toward the surface plane and the viewer. *Beetles* (shown below), by professional silk painter Ellen Tobey-Holmes, clearly illustrates this. The images that are closest to us have more detail and vibrant color, while the overpainted images fade into the dark recesses of the painting. This process of successive applications of dye and then resist creates the depth and is referred to as layering.

Layering is not one specific technique but a combination of various aspects of silk painting. Here, Ellen used a linear underpainting at the start of this work, but also incorporated shading, blending, and overpainting methods to create a finished piece.

She also uses the color blue as a common hue to tie the painting together and provide added atmosphere.

Note that the dyes you choose for this technique should move on the silk when nudged with alcohol diluent. As discussed in chapter 1, the dyes that work best for these silk painting techniques are those that do not strike the fabric on contact. In this way, the dye can be easily manipulated and various painterly and textural effects can be achieved. It is also important to work with a gutta rather than a water-based resist, because gutta is much stronger and will better tolerate the alcohol diluent and layerings of color.

BEETLES. © Ellen Tobey-Holmes. *This silk painting was executed with a linear underpainting as a base. Guidelines for using an underpainting to achieve this type of effect are provided in the demonstration that begins on the next page.*

DEMONSTRATION:
Linear Underpainting and Layering

This demonstration piece was executed by Ellen Tobey-Holmes. During my week-long workshop at the Peters Valley Craft Center, Ellen learned the underpainting and dye-layering techniques she illustrates here.

The linear outline of the motif is first drawn on the silk with a blue EZ Wash Out pencil (also available in white for drawing on a colored ground). Used by dressmakers and quilters, these pencils can be found in any fabric shop.

Using a Black Velvet brush, Ellen then applies the linear underpainting of dye over the drawing. Give careful thought to your color choices at this stage, because these hues provide the foundation on which you will build the form in your composition. This foundation will be more effective if the colors of your linear underpainting are shades and tones of those you plan to use in your painting. Brighter colors introduce a strong design element that may be difficult to coordinate and blend with your motifs.

After the dye dries, clear gutta resist is applied over the colored lines of the underpainting. When doing this, it is not necessary to cover the entire width of the lines, which will naturally be broad and uneven; just follow them and apply the gutta in an even manner. Make sure that the gutta penetrates through to the back of the silk; if it does not, it may be that your silk is still damp from the underpainting. (Remember, resists will not penetrate wet silk.) However, if your silk is dry and the gutta still will not penetrate it, thin the gutta down with a few drops of thinner (mineral spirits). Test the new resist mix on a scrap of silk before proceeding.

After the gutta is applied, edges of the linear underpainting will remain uncovered on either side of the resist line. Ellen removes or softens these edges with alcohol diluent. To do this, apply the diluent to the outside edges of the underpainting with a brush. The diluent will crawl toward the resist line, dislodging the dye and pushing it up against the gutta line. You can use a small Silverwhite brush to rub the silk and assist the alcohol diluent in loosening the dye. Use a cotton swab to carefully lift and remove the diluent and dislodged dye. Note: It is not critical that all the color be removed; the remaining halo of dye can be worked into your painting and may ultimately make the finished piece more painterly. Ellen has left a bit of a halo here.

Ellen adds the dye to the motifs, and while it is still wet she blends it using a round Black Velvet brush. The delicate details and blending are executed with small, round Silverwhite brushes. The dark dots on the light areas of the bug are made with carefully placed spots of dye. In the darker areas, dots of alcohol diluent are applied to the silk to push the dye away, creating light spots; the result is a ring of dye around a dot of lighter color.

The flat background color is laid down. To avoid streaking when applying a flat ground, work quickly, overlapping the edges of the brushstrokes as you move across and down the silk. It is easy to avoid streaking in smaller areas such as these because the brushstrokes are short. For larger background areas, which are more difficult to paint because the dye dries so quickly, use a background blender or a large, squirrel-hair quill brush (see chapter 1). In either situation, as long as the area is still wet, you can go back over streaks and further dissolve and rub-blend the dye to even it out.

The next two steps illustrate how depth and space can be created in a design by layering images and dye applications. On the painted background, Ellen draws an outline of leaf shapes in gutta. Before applying more dye, Ellen chooses a few leaves that will be lighter than the others and removes some of their background color dye. (For this she uses a small Silverwhite brush and alcohol diluent, which dislodges the dye from the silk; she then picks up the dislodged color with a cotton swab, as recommended in the fourth step.) When first painting over a background color, you may feel as though you are painting in the dark with no guidelines and no definition to the forms, but once the dye dries you will be amazed at the richness and depth of the color. With experience you will be better able to control the color effects.

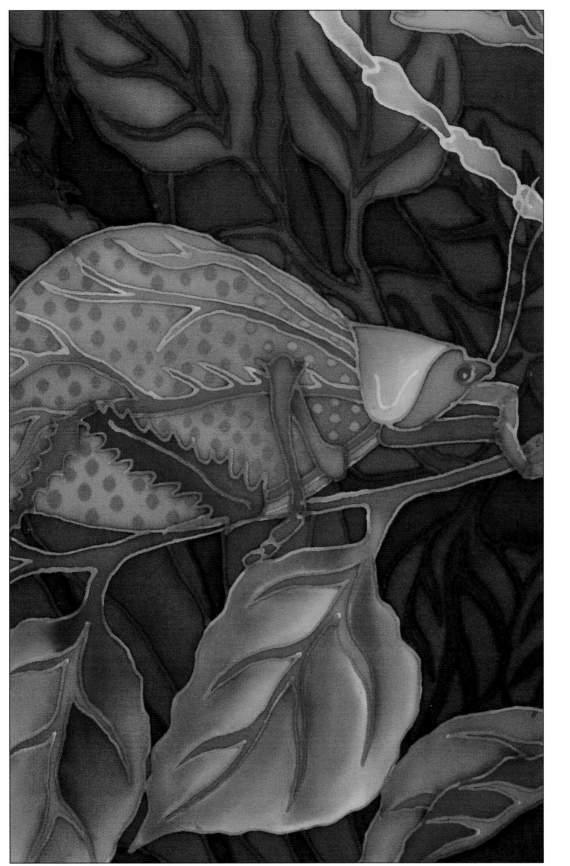

In the second layering step, Ellen paints another color over the background. She then draws more leaf outlines (over this new color) with gutta resist, filling some in with more dye and leaving others unpainted. She also applies yet another background color to silhouette and really define the unpainted leaves. Notice in the complete painting on page 85, how once the clear gutta is dry-cleaned out, the resist line around the unpainted leaves does not show.

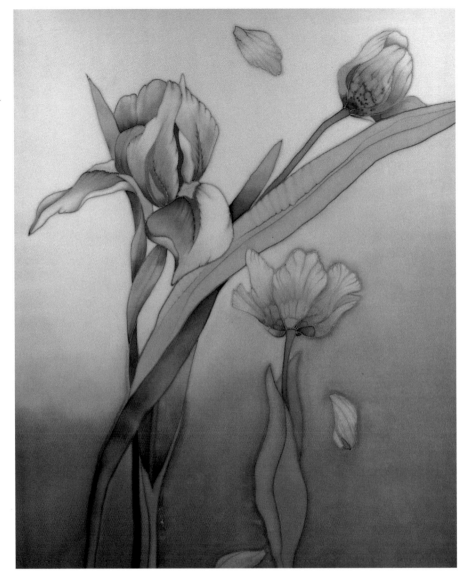

FLOWERS FOR ARLENE. © Susan L. Moyer. *In this commissioned piece, the dyes were mixed to coordinate with the color harmonies and decor of an already furnished room. To give the painting added presence, violet (a color not found in the room) was used to create a split-complementary color scheme involving both the artwork and the room. Several tones of these chosen colors were also applied in the linear underpainting.*

FLOWERS FOR ARLENE (detail of the work in progress). © Susan L. Moyer. *In this sample that I made for teaching purposes, alcohol diluent and a blow drier were used to move dye and create the form of the delicate petals and leaves. The wet diluent lifted and moved the dry dye, creating ridges of concentrated color. Once the ridges were in place, the blow drier was used to dry the silk and further control the flow of dye.*

PALE BELL ORCHIDS. © Suzanne Punch. *This painting shows the beautiful results that can be created by using alcohol diluent to move and blend the edges of a linear underpainting into the motifs and the background.*

EVANGELINE (detail). © Suzanne Punch. *An experienced silk painter, Suzanne blends the linear underpainting into her composition to achieve a painterly feel in her motifs.*

7 WAX RESIST TECHNIQUES

The process of using melted wax and dye for fabric decoration is a technique that predates recorded history. Wax was applied to cloth in order to repel dye, while the unwaxed areas received color by immersion in dye baths. Over time, many different cultures developed their own wax resist techniques, each complete with their own unique tools, wax recipes, dyes, and methods of application. There are the more basic, time-honored batik methods from the island of Java, and there is also the more recent Japanese *roketsu-zome* technique. While I find it very informative, inspirational, and conducive to my own artistic growth to study and periodically reexamine these various tools, processes, and traditions, in this chapter I will focus primarily on the roketsu-zome method, which can inspire new and diverse techniques and very beautiful results for the silk painter.

UNTITLED (detail). © Ina Kozel

MATERIALS AND TOOLS FOR WAX RESIST TECHNIQUES

Wax is a highly effective resist material. When melted, it becomes very fluid and easy to apply, and there are many different types. There are also a variety of tools with which to apply wax to silk.

Basic Waxes

Paraffin. This is a white or clear wax that is a petroleum by-product. Its melting point is anywhere between 120°F and 145° F. When applied to silk, it cools to a hard, smooth, clear resist. This even surface makes it easy to see and wipe off any dye residue, if necessary. When dry, it is brittle and cracks easily.

Microcrystalline. Also referred to as micro-wax, this petroleum by-product has a light brown, nutty color and is often used cold by artists for modelmaking and sculpting. It has a melting point of anywhere from 160°F to 180° F, and when applied to the silk, it cools into a flexible resist that won't easily crack. However, unlike paraffin, even when cool it has a slightly sticky surface. This makes it difficult to clean off any unwanted dye residue from the wax. It is also difficult to apply to and remove from fabric. Therefore, it is primarily mixed with other waxes for its flexible, crack-inhibiting qualities.

Beeswax. Beeswax is a natural substance collected from the honeycombs of beehives, which comes in its natural color (yellow) and a bleached version (white). It has a lower melting point(136° F) than microcrystalline wax, but a slightly higher one than the paraffin. Both flexible and thick, beeswax does not spread out of control as easily as other waxes. It tends to hold its resist line when applied. Although expensive, many artists use it exclusively because they feel it emits fewer dangerous fumes than the petroleum waxes.

Mokuro. This is a natural, light yellow-green wax from the Japanese haze tree. It has a low melting point and a sticky texture. It is easy to paint with and penetrates the silk well, but on its own it is not a strong resist and so it is usually combined with other more tenacious waxes.

Hakuro. Hakuro is the bleached, slightly harder version of mokuro.

Waxes for Special Effects

Stearin. This is a Chinese wax made from the harder ingredients of the fatty by-products of plants (tallow from the Chinese tallow tree) and animals (both suet and tallow). It is used to create soft, cracked lines such as those achieved in batik.

Wax-balm. Also called carnauba wax, this is a yellow wax from the leaves of the South American carnauba palm tree (*Copernicia cerifera*). This wax is most commonly used as a furniture wax, but in some roketsu-zome techniques it is used to create hard cracked lines that look very fractured. This is done by removing the wax-encrusted silk from its stretcher and crumpling it, cracking the wax.

Ryudo paraffin. This liquid wax can be ordered through most drug stores and chemical supply outlets and is added to other wax formulas to retard cooling and control dripping.

In the foreground are three Silver Econo Gesso brushes, two with their bristles cut and shaped to add special effects and texture. To the left is a Japanese ro-fude brush and a Silverstone fan brush. Above this is a cut sponge brush and one of Keith Lebenzon's handmade bamboo-handle brushes. (Keep hot wax brushes from sticking to a surface by placing them on wax paper as pictured.) At top left is a Rabinowitz Wax Melter Electric Batik Pen. At top right is a Handi-Pan with blocks of beeswax and paraffin.

On the left is a Japanese jizomebake, made of deer hair, that is used for dyeing large areas and backgrounds; next to it is a peony brush, which is also used for shading and blending of dye.

Melting Wax

There are many ways to melt wax, but the safest method is to use an electric skillet with a built-in temperature gauge. I use a small Handi-Pan manufactured by Toastmaster. A small pan is stable and easily accommodates any less-expansive work surfaces. Also with a smaller pan, any brushes that you leave resting on the edges won't slide down into the melted wax. If you are using a larger pan and find that your brushes do slip into the wax, place a clean rock in the bottom of the pan. This will block their fall. You can also cut the bottom out of a shallow can and use the ring for this, too. It is a good idea not to leave your brushes in the wax pot for long periods of time as they can burn and become frizzy.

When working with more than one type of wax, you can heat them all in the same pot while keeping them separate by first placing the individual, unmelted waxes in shallow cans. Put the cans into the pot and begin heating. Once melted, wax should be kept at between 250°F and 260°F. If the wax starts to smoke excessively, it is too hot. Check your pot; the temperature control may be defective. When working with melted wax always ventilate your work area and wear a surgical mask; hot wax often emits strong fumes that can irritate nasal passages.

Brushes and Tools

Wax can be applied to silk in a variety of ways. Traditional processes include using tjanting tools, tjap stamps, and brushes, which have all evolved over time. The tjanting tool is a drawing tool for applying wax in fine lines (as with any linear resist). Hot wax is poured into a metal receptacle and then flows through a spout onto the silk. The spouts are available in different sizes to achieve a variety of wax-line widths. Hand-held electric tjanting tools and Waxmelter Batik Pens are also available; they also create durable, fine wax resist lines that will withstand repeated applications of diluent and dye. A tjap stamp is a seal made from a heat conducting material that is used to imprint an image in wax on the silk.

Brushes will add a more spontaneous stroke to the wax application. Larger brushes are more appropriate, because they hold more wax and maintain the heat longer in their bristles. You can even cut the bristles of your wax brushes to achieve more unusual designs and textures in your wax application. For example, an uneven bristle edge might allow you to paint an interesting pattern of stripes of wax. The traditional Japanese *ro-fude* brush is a good choice, especially since it has a heat-resistant, bamboo handle. An excellent alternative to this is a plump, round sable watercolor brush that comes to a fine point. Note that most sable watercolor rounds have metal ferrules that will need to be insulated with several layers of masking tape before being used. They become hot very quickly and will burn your hands if left uncovered.

When you are introducing a new natural-hair brush to hot wax, repeatedly dip it into the mixture for a few seconds at a

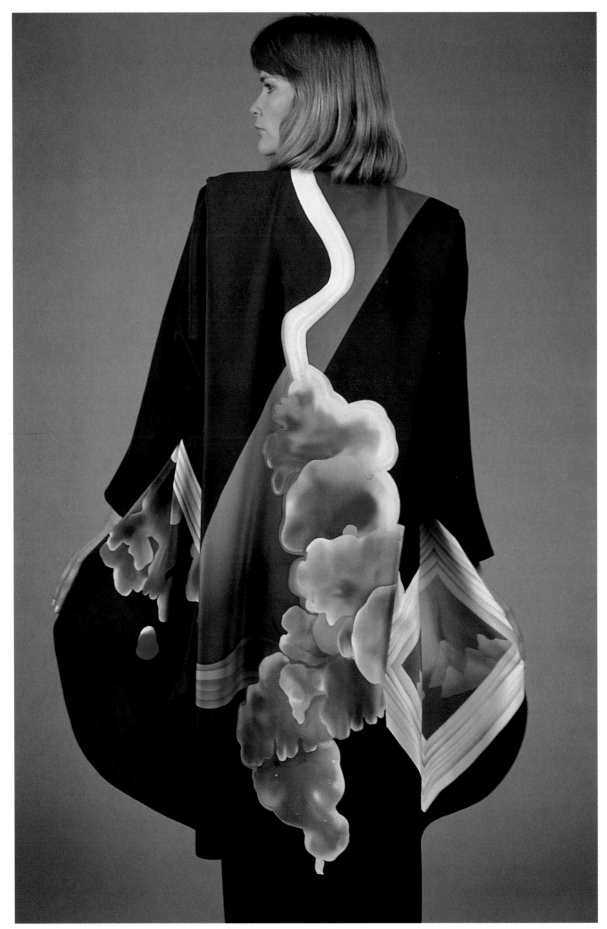

UNTITLED. © Ina Kozel. *Here, Ina contrasts shape and color to add drama to her wearable art; the juxtaposition of the organic yellow shape against a violet geometric one is very striking.*

These are various sizes of the Japanese brush (bokashi-bake) used for graduated shading and blending of dye.

time, or stroke the new brush with a previously used brush containing hot wax. This will "temper" the brush and help prevent the hairs from curling and becoming brittle. Avoid leaving a ro-fude brush standing in the hot pan. Before allowing the wax to cool, remove your brushes from the wax, stroke them into a point, and let them cool on wax paper.

When choosing a natural-hair brush for wax drawing and masking, look for quality. Select one that gives you excellent control. Although you will need much practice to become skilled at applying wax, a second-rate brush will make wax drawing and masking endlessly difficult.

Of course, you will also need your brushes for dye application, but these should be kept separate from your wax brushes. Do not confuse them. Wax is impossible to remove, so brushes with wax in them are not really cleaned; they are simply allowed to cool and harden. The hard wax in them softens up with the heat of the next application. So your dye brushes should remain exclusively for dyes, and your wax brushes for wax.

Wax Formulas

The following are various wax formulas that silk painter and instructor Betsy Sterling Benjamin uses for the Japanese *roketsu-zome* technique, which is described on the following pages. Since some of the waxes are hard to locate in the U.S., she has also provided alternative mixtures.

Formulas for Traditional Roketsu-Zome

I have provided two versions for each formula, to accommodate varying weather conditions and room temperatures.

		summer hot and humid	winter cold and dry
Formula 1:	mokuro (or hakuro)	70%	60%
	paraffin	30%	40%
Formula 2:	paraffin	70%	40%
	micro-wax	30%	60%
	mokuro (or hakuro)	some	some
	Ryudo paraffin	some	some

For a better, more flexible resist and to prevent the wax application from cracking, add some micro-wax to the first formula. For summer: 58% mokuro/hakuro, 25% paraffin, 17% micro-wax. For winter: 50% mokuro, 33% paraffin, 17% micro-wax.

Alternative Formulas for Roketsu-Zome

These alternate formulas (also from Betsy) are used by silk painters Ina Kozel, Dorte Christjansen, Roberta Glidden, and myself. The first is Ina's standard formula.

Formula 1:	beeswax	50%
	paraffin	50%
Formula 2:	beeswax	80%
	micro-wax or paraffin	20%

Note that the micro-wax will make the second formula thicker, and the paraffin will make it thinner. Also, there are no variations for weather or temperature for these.

ROKETSU-ZOME

When I took part in a workshop at the National Surface Design Conference at the University of Seattle, I was introduced to a Japanese resist technique called *roketsu-zome* by Betsy Sterling Benjamin, a Kyoto-based fiber artist who specializes in this method of applying wax and dye. Betsy has also written a comprehensive book entitled *The World of Rozome: Wax Resist Textiles of Japan,* published by Kodansha International. This informative book teaches the finer points of the traditional Japanese wax resist techniques and beautifully illustrates the history of rozome (wax resist techniques) as well as the work of contemporary Japanese roketsu-zome artists.

In this resist process, wax is applied to areas of a design that are to be saved, forming a durable resist. The painting procedure continues with alternating applications of dye and wax. While realizing that I would need years of practice and instruction to become a master roketsu-zome artist like Betsy, my way of thinking about and planning silk paintings was greatly expanded by her teachings.

Wax Application and Brushes

In traditional roketsu-zome methods, which are utilized by the kimono industry, wax is used primarily as a masking agent, much as a frisket is used with airbrush techniques. To mask an area, wax is applied to the silk with a *ro-fude* brush made of sheep hair. It is placed first on the backside of the dry silk (covering any already-painted areas—as with any resist), and then the second and third layers of wax are applied on the frontside, over the same spots. More than one layer of wax is used to ensure a strong resist and smooth surface so that dyes do not touch the silk and any excess can be easily and thoroughly wiped off the hard wax surface.

This even wax coverage is maintained by controlling the temperature of the wax (keeping it warm enough to be easily manipulated) and by working quickly to prevent the outside, or leading, edges of wax from becoming cold before the application process is finished. If this process is interrupted and the leading edges harden prematurely, the resist coverage will not penetrate the silk properly and evenly. There may be subtle separations at the points where you stopped and then started the wax application, and the dye will collect in these grooves or recesses. Dye will settle in even the slightest crevices in the wax surface and will ultimately create unwanted textures in the design during the wax removal or steam-fixing process, when the dye becomes deposited on the silk.

Therefore, traditional artists never outline a shape in wax and then fill in the center because the outline may become visible

GAIA SUITE: FERN. © Betsy Sterling Benjamin. *Betsy works in the traditional roketsu-zome and bokashi techniques to create her subtly blended backgrounds. The texture in the ground was created by spraying wax onto the silk between dye applications.*

once the dye is applied and seeps into the resulting crack. Instead, the brushstrokes are feathered in from the edge of a form; they are slightly overlapped to ensure that any cooler edges of wax are still warm, melted, and blended together. To apply wax in small areas, use only the tip of the brush; to cover broader areas, utilize the entire brush, including the wider part of the bristles (the belly). When you apply the second layer, place the wax slightly inside the outside edges of the first layer, taking care not to overflow those edges, thereby creating a ridge in which the dye may collect.

Kimono-fabric painters using the roketsu-zome technique must take great care with wax application because kimono manufacturers have such high standards of perfection for the fabrics they use. Successful wax application takes experience and a complete understanding of the different properties of each type of wax, but with dedicated practice it can be mastered.

Dyes

The concentrated liquid dyes that many Japanese roketsu-zome artists use are prepared from acid premetallized powdered dyes. Before painting with these dyes, Japanese artists size (or treat) their fabric with a soybean liquid and water mixture called *gojiru*. The gojiru acts as a natural, mild stop-flow, bonding the dyes to the silk and preventing them from migrating and streaking excessively, and it also helps to fully develop dye colors. It should be applied to the prewashed silk and allowed to dry before you proceed with the painting. If you use liquid acid dyes (either Pébéo, H. Dupont, or Tinfix), you do not need the gojiru to bring out the colors because they will come out fully during the steam-fixing process. However, they will streak less and be even more workable if they are combined with a bit of the manufacturer's diluent or a touch of Ivory Liquid soap or Synthrapol. If you are very concerned about the liquid dyes migrating and streaking, due to the repeated applications of wax and dye involved in the roketsu-zome process, you can size the silk with a thin coat of gojiru.

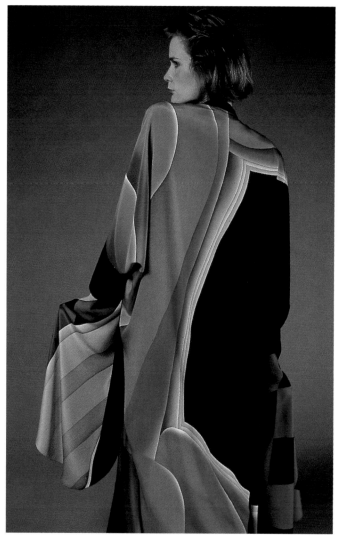

UNTITLED. © Ina Kozel. *The sweeping, organic shapes and complementary color scheme played against the black make a bold, dramatic statement in this garment.*

Gojiru Recipe

This gojiru recipe, which yields ½ gallon, is adapted from the video *Japanese Textile Dyeing with John Marshall,* from A/Zo Production.

½ cup or more of dry soybeans

2-cup container or bowl

½ gallon of water

large bowl

colander that fits inside the large bowl

small bowl

cheese cloth

blender

Place the soybeans in the 2-cup container. Cover with water and soak overnight (the water should completely cover the beans). They will expand to approximately 1 cup, so make

sure you use a container that can accommodate this increase. Drain the beans and then place them and the water in the blender and blend at a high speed. Place the cheese cloth in the colander and put the colander in the large bowl. Pour the soybean mixture into the cheese cloth, gather up the sides of the cloth, and squeeze out the liquid, which is the soy milk, into the small bowl and set aside.

Return the soy pulp (left in the cheese cloth) to the blender, add the remaining water, and repeat the process, squeezing the additional soy milk into the small bowl. Repeat the process another two or three times, using the strained soy milk as the liquid for grinding.

This soy milk is gojiru and once you have collected the liquid from a few repetitions, you should have enough to apply to the fabric. For roketsu-zome, the consistency and translucency of the soy milk should match that of skim milk. If it looks like cream, add more water; if it is too thin, add more presoaked and ground soybeans.

Dye Application and Brushes

The brushwork technique usually employed in the roketsu-zome method is *bokashi*. It involves the graduated shading and blending of dye in a circular rubbing motion with a dry brush on silk that has been wet with water, and it is synonymous with most types of Japanese dyeing. Bokashi results in deep, rich color, but since the silk is damp, the dyes should be used in a more concentrated form so that the color does not become too diluted and light when it is placed on the saturated fabric.

To apply the dyes in this manner, special, bamboo-handle brushes are used. The *bokashi-bake* is a soft brush with short, dense bristles (of deer or badger hair) that have been secured into a full, flat-edged oval or round shape similar to that of a stencil brush. It is used for dry-brush blending on a wet ground. The *botan-bake,* or peony brush, is intended for a wetter application of dye because it has a round-shaped edge (rather than a flat, hard one) that prevents uneven applications and streaking. It is also used for shading and blending. The larger *jizomome-bake,* or ground-coloring brush, also has a round edge and is used for backgrounds. I have also found these unique brushes, and the bokashi technique, to be an excellent means of creating areas of blended color (mixing dark to light shades and one color into another) when using other silk painting techniques.

Unfortunately, these hand-crafted Japanese brushes are becoming more difficult to locate because young apprentices are no longer learning the craft of specialty brushmaking.

Bokashi Dye Application Technique

In the traditional roketsu-zome bokashi technique you work wet-on-wet, applying the dye to dampened silk. Areas of dye that are to be saved are covered with wax, and then concentrated dye is placed on the edges of the wax and blended and graduated on the silk in a circular rubbing motion with a slightly damp bokashi-bake.

Before any dye is applied, the fabric is treated with gojiru. After this has dried, dampen the silk with water using a sponge. If the painting is in progress and contains areas already painted but not protected with wax, wet the work quickly so the dye won't streak. Begin your painting, let it dry, then cover elements to be saved with wax. After this wax has cooled, wipe it clean and dry. Then place beads of concentrated dye on the wax, near its edges.

Using a damp bokashi-bake, blend the color into the wet silk to achieve a graduated, dark-to-light effect. Use the circular rubbing motion for this.

You can obtain a richer color by again placing more dots of dye on the wax edge and blending them into the silk. Avoid streaks of concentrated dye in lighter-colored areas by always blending gradually from dark to light, and blotting the brush on a clean paper towel. After blending, wipe the wax clean of dye. After the silk has dried, apply the wax to new areas you want to save, let it cool, and continue.

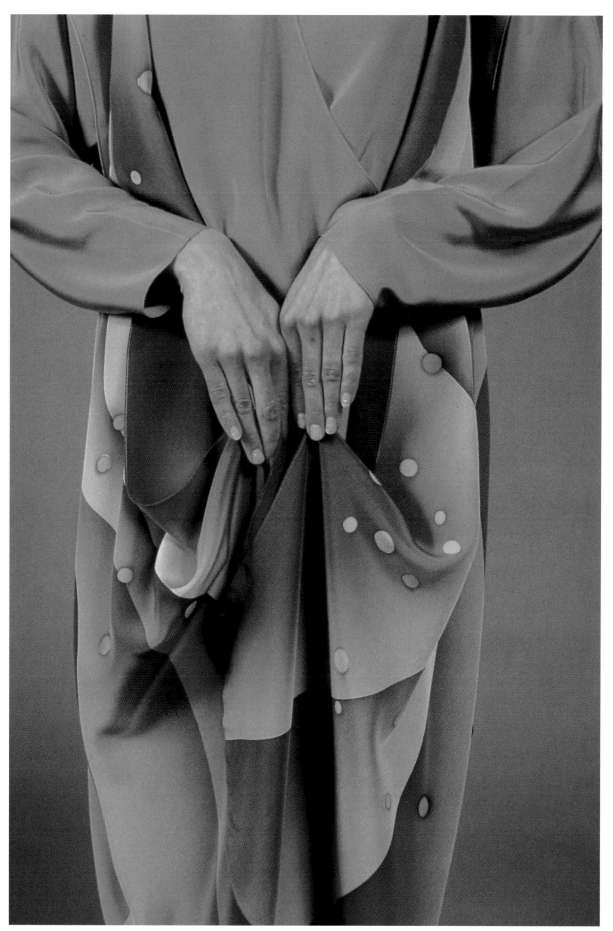

UNTITLED (detail). © Ina Kozel. *Ina worked with the traditional roketsu-zome and bokashi techniques to create the transitions of serene tones accented with bright blue-green dots seen here.*

EXPLORATIONS AND ADAPTATIONS

It takes logic, concentration, and experience to compose and execute wax resist paintings. The numerous applications of dye and wax on the fabric eventually result in multiple layers of form and a strong sense of depth in a composition. Once these skills become internalized, this knowledge will enable faster, more spontaneous expression through the medium of silk painting.

After applying some of the Japanese tools and techniques to my own silk painting, I began to notice how other painters, like Ina Kozel, Roberta Glidden, and Dorte Christjansen, have been directly or indirectly influenced by roketsu-zome. Ina, an artist who studied roketsu-zome in Kyoto and has an extensive background in painting, has developed her own, very untraditional approach to applying wax and dye. She has taken the essence of these techniques—bokashi blending brushwork, and layering of dye and wax to build form—and put them together with an intuitive understanding of her materials. Her wearable art (reproduced on the preceding pages) directly reflects the fluidity of the wax and her medium, and the spontaneous spirit of her involvement with them.

Roberta Glidden, who also attended Betsy Sterling Benjamin's workshop, has been especially diligent about exploring roketsu-zome and has used it to develop her own unique representational style. Focusing her imagery on the plants and landscapes of the West, Roberta finds that through the roketsu-zome process she is able to build more form in her paintings and create a greater sense of depth than with the usual linear resist associated with silk painting techniques (see the demonstration that follows). This method works for her visually, and she also finds the skill, concentration, and practice that the process demands to be particularly rewarding.

Dorte Christjansen, a teacher at California State University, Fullerton, who has a B.A. in drawing and painting and an M.A. in illustration, has been indirectly influenced by roketsu-zome. Her process (also highlighted in a demonstrations in this section) does not embrace the traditional bokashi techniques for shading and blending dye (nor the wax application techniques of roketsu-zome), yet her paintings still reflect the multi-layering of dye that she uses to build form and depth. She applies her wax with round sable watercolor brushes and tjanting tools and applies her dyes with plastic spray bottles, and Black Velvet round brushes mentioned in chapter 1, which she finds excellent for blending. Inspired by the natural beauty of her home state, she finds her garden to be a major source of inspiration and imagery and has compiled sketchbooks full of ideas and compositions. In fact, she treats her garden as a living painting, planting for color and textural variations, which frequently surface in her compositions.

FALLEN LEAVES. © Roberta Glidden. Photo by the artist. *In this surface design, Roberta very effectively creates form and texture. The dry leaf effect was created by brushing in wax leaf outlines and then filling them in with more wax. Applying the wax in this uneven but methodical way catches the dye, creating texture and interest. A tjanting tool was used to suggest veins and highlights on the leaves.*

DEMONSTRATION: Creating a Sense of Depth

A silk painting teacher in the continuing education program at the University of Utah, Roberta Glidden put together this step-by-step demonstration to illustrate how she created her painting *Picked a Pile of Peppers* (right). Drawing on her extensive background in commercial surface design, she covers the basic procedures of how she builds a painting. She uses the natural bleed of dyes applied to wet fabric to add a sense of depth to this piece; when the shape of the motif (here peppers) is then waxed, the bled color remains exposed and is used to suggest shadows.

PICKED A PILE OF PEPPERS. © Roberta Glidden. Photo by the artist.

The drawing is traced or drawn on the back of the stretched silk with a soft lead pencil. The frame is then turned over and, with a sponge, the front of the piece is wet evenly with water or alcohol diluent. Once wet, the lines appear clearly on the front side. Working wet-on-wet on the front side, green dye is applied to some of the stem shapes, and the silk is allowed to dry thoroughly. Then the painting is turned to the back side again (where the drawing is still visible) and the green stems are covered with wax.

The front of the silk is again wet with a sponge to make the drawing lines visible. Still on the front and working from the waxed areas outward, gold and yellow dyes are applied and blended on three peppers. The fabric is allowed to dry thoroughly, the painting is again turned to the back, and the peppers are covered with wax. (Note: As the painting progresses, this set of peppers will appear on the top of the pile.)

The front is again sponged, and a second layer of pepper shapes are painted using a red-orange color. Again, they are allowed to dry and are then waxed on the back side. (This layer of peppers will appear behind the first.)

Following these procedures, red dye is applied, blended, and shaded on the third layer of peppers, then dried and waxed.

A slightly deeper red is applied, blended, and shaded on the fourth layer of peppers, then dried and waxed.

Finally, the blue background is painted on the unwaxed areas. After the silk dries, Roberta covers the entire piece with wax to prevent migration of the dye during steaming.

DORTE CHRISTJANSEN'S WAX RESIST TECHNIQUE

Through continual exploration of wax resist techniques, Dorte Christjansen has developed a unique approach that involves multiple layerings of wax and dye. For fabric, she prefers a silk with a smooth, even weave that doesn't interfere with her images. The result is a painting style of great beauty, complexity, and subtlety.

Wax Formula and Application

Dorte uses a wax formulated from 50 percent microcrystalline and 50 percent paraffin. When this wax is applied over a color, it creates a muddy, yellow cast, which eventually disappears when the wax is removed from the silk. Dorte suggests painting color swatches of each dye so that you will still be able to make informed color choices when your work becomes covered with and temporarily distorted by the wax. She also suggests that you periodically hold your work-in-progress up to the light to better see underlying colors.

To apply the wax to larger areas, Dorte employs various sable watercolor rounds, which she uses expressly for wax. To ensure that the wax on the brush is always hot enough to deposit a clean stroke and penetrate the silk, she leaves 10 to 12 brushes in the electric wax skillet and rotates their use. She also uses an electric tjanting tool (the Rabinowitz Wax Melter Electric Batik Pen) for outlining and hatching. When working with an electric tjanting, Dorte stresses that to control spills and wax flow, you should fill the tjanting only partway. She also suggests keeping a rag or paper towel handy to hold underneath the tool as you carry it across your work and for any blotting that might be necessary. Of course, you should practice your application technique beforehand as well.

Dyes and Color Palette

Dorte has developed her own basic palette by compiling a variety of compatible silk dyes that she blends to make many beautiful colors. She uses these concentrated stock dyes (concentrated liquid dyes), which are mixed from acid dye powders, and supplements them with compatible H. Dupont, Sennelier, and Pébéo dyes. Her formula for mixing a color from dye powder is as follows: 1 teaspoon dye, 1 teaspoon Calgon (a powdered water softener), 1 tablespoon vinegar, 1 cup boiling hot water. Note that you should place the dye first in only a small amount of the boiling water and then add the remaining water. The Calgon will make the dye move more evenly on the silk.

Dorte's palette consists of these stock colors: canary yellow, turquoise, magenta (a hot pink), vermilion red, maroon (a rich, plummy raspberry), ultramarine, emerald green (a brilliant green), gray blue-green (a teal), red-violet, violet, and black.

Painting Technique

Dorte uses small glass containers to hold her dyes. To them she adds the necessary alcohol diluent to create the desired tints. She uses an assortment of brushes and, when working on large pieces, she often sprays dyes onto the silk with plastic spray bottles. She controls the concentration of the spray both by varying the distance of the spray bottle to the fabric and by working alternately with sprays of dye and alcohol diluent (her diluent mixture is ⅔ alcohol to ⅓ water).

An aggressive painter, Dorte fires away with both hands to

create specked textures, splatters, and gradations. Sometimes she even places the framed silk in a vertical position (as if working upright on an easel), letting the dye drip down the fabric and then rotating the frame so there is a change in the direction of the drips and different colors blend together.

Occasionally, when working with wax resist, spots of dye that are left to dry on the wax may eventually seep through it and stain the fabric, or they may inadvertently dye the silk during any setting processes. This dye will discolor whatever pigment it touches, adding a textural effect that may or may not be desired. If Dorte does not want this effect, she immediately wipes the wet dye off the waxed areas with a damp rag or cotton swab (a technique suggested previously in this section). She also finds that, as her work progresses, the wax resist sometimes breaks down under the repeated applications of dye and alcohol. When this occurs she waits for her painting to dry and touches up the wax application so that it continues to resist the dye.

PRIMAVERA. (detail) © Dorte Christjansen. *Dorte designed this unique, kaleidoscopic arrangement of garden flowers by combining many of her detailed sketches and drawings.*

SUNFLOWERS. (detail). © Dorte Christjansen. *Dorte controls the cracking of the wax application in her complex compositions by rewaxing any areas where the cracking interferes with the design and drawing.*

EPI III. © 1989 Dorte Christjansen. *This floral subject and surrounding border design were executed using Dorte's unique wax resist methods (see following demonstrations).*

CALLA LILY FIELD (detail). © Dorte Christjansen. *Again, Dorte used her drawing skills and her wax resist techniques intuitively to create this spontaneous field of flowers.*

DEMONSTRATION:
Dorte Christjansen's Wax Resist Technique

I asked Dorte to analyze her complex wax resist painting *Calla Lily Field* (a detail of which appears on the preceding page) and explain each technical step and thought process involved in its development. She created this demonstration as a result.

Dorte first draws the outlines of her composition on white paper with a black felt-tipped pen. When she transfers the drawing to silk, this heavy pen line will be easily visible through the silk.

After stretching the silk taut on the Moyer Design Fabric Stretching System, Dorte tapes the paper to the underside of the silk. She places a piece of ½-inch foam board, which fits inside the stretcher, under the stretched silk so that the design is pressed up against the fabric and can be seen through it. Then she traces the design (following these outlines) onto the silk with a regular soft (2B or 4B) pencil. Once finished, she removes the foam board and drawing from the silk and lifts the frame onto its legs so that the fabric is suspended above the work surface for the wax and dye applications.

With her first application of wax onto the unpainted ground, she saves any white areas that she wants to use later as highlights. These highlights will also establish movement in the composition. The linear areas of wax outline the main shapes and thereby control the flow of dye in the painting. At this point, Dorte also puts down her first application of dye (a linear underpainting), and here she uses tints, shades, and diluted washes of various yellow, red, and green hues. While working, Dorte periodically wets the silk with a spray of alcohol diluent.

With the second application of wax, Dorte defines the details in the leaves and calla lilies. She does this by drawing a series of linear brushstrokes with the wax (these appear as deep yellow lines because the wax is an unbleached, golden yellow). She concentrates the light effects mainly on the three lilies in the lower left corner of the painting and will later introduce shadows with applications of darker dye. Keeping composition in mind, Dorte has begun to lay the foundation for the diagonal movement, which will be seen in some of the white lilies amongst the darker leaves.

Dorte is now ready for her second application of dye. Dorte keeps the silk moist with an occasional spray of alcohol diluent and, working wet-on-wet (as with the bokashi technique), she intensifies the previously applied greens and yellows by adding more of these hues. She then utilizes a split-complementary color scheme by introducing violet, red-violet, and magenta to the greens. After the dyes are fairly dry, Dorte sprays a light mist of diluted magenta (hot pink) and teal green hues onto the painting to build textural effects. Once the silk is completely dry, additional leaf and stem forms are drawn and saved with wax, creating depth and enriching the background with pattern.

On the third application of wax and dye, Dorte continues building form with layering. She completely covers the top five lilies with wax and fills in most of the leaves, leaving exposed only those areas that are to receive dark accents. To emulate the feeling of depth and sunlight found in her gardens, Dorte contrasts the white of the liles with darker ultramarine blue and red-violet accents. As the painting dries, she sprays it again with both the diluted teal green hue and the hot pink, occasionally overlapping the applications. To soften the original white highlights on the leaves (saved in the third step), Dorte repeatedly paints dyes over the wax until the color penetrates through to the silk, leaving a slight haze of color on the fabric.

With the second layer of wax, Dorte used hatching and brushwork to define the surface contours of the lilies and leaves. To further define the images, she now fills in the narrow, unwaxed spaces, which outline some of the shapes, with dye. To create more depth in the centers of the lilies, Dorte left them unwaxed and here paints them a deep purple.

Red-violet, violet, and blue-green were applied to the veins of the leaves. Dorte used a very wet brush to apply a color at each end of the leaf vein. The colors flowed between the lines creating gradations where the two colors met. This technique added form to the leaves. Throughout the painting an atmosphere of depth and shadow was created by using blue as a common hue.

To prepare the painting for its fifth and final application of dye (which will be black), Dorte fills in all the remaining shapes and spaces with wax, except for the defining outlines, which she wants to receive the black dye. She also reinforces previously waxed areas with fresh wax or carefully reheats them with the spout of the electric wax tool to seal and bind any cracks or thinner areas. Since the black dye is strong and corrosive, Dorte applies it directly into the unwaxed areas and then immediately wipes it off the wax so that any excess dye does not stain through or eat away at the wax seal. Note that at this stage, the painting appears dull and yellowish from all the layers of wax.

Now Dorte removes the thick layer of wax from the silk. She irons out most of the wax before the painting is steam-fixed. Once the painting is free of the yellow cast of the wax, its true colors are revealed along with all the strong juxtaposition of highlights and dark recesses. Now you can clearly see the diagonal movement and sense of depth created by the contrasting light liles against the darker, receding stems and leaves. The textures created throughout by the layers of hatching and dye convey Dorte's unique style and add interest and form to the images. For instruction on wax removal, refer to the alcohol discharge demonstration on pages 114–115. Directions for steam fixing are provided in chapter 9.

ALCOHOL TECHNIQUES

Used to execute my painting on the cover of this book, the alcohol discharge technique allows color placement effects that would not otherwise be possible. One way to use alcohol (either pure or diluted with water) is to place droplets of it on a painted silk ground. As it spreads into a spot on the fabric, the alcohol pushes the dye to the outer edge of that shape, creating a thin ring of darker color there. When dry, the spot will remain lighter than the ground color and the outer ring at its edge will be slightly darker. Basically, you are using the alcohol to manipulate the dye, and a variety of interesting textures and painterly effects can be achieved. For example, you can apply brushstrokes of alcohol diluent rather than droplets. If you use this method, it is best to let the painted ground dry thoroughly before applying any alcohol, because the effect of moving the color is more pronounced when the dye is dry.

Diluted alcohol can also be applied as a wash to unpainted silk prior to beginning a painting. This wet-on-wet technique causes the subsequently applied dyes to flow and spread more slowly and dry with a softer edge than they would on silk without an alcohol wash. As in the following demonstration, this technique can be combined with wax resist effects to create and integrate contrasting textures into one overall design. The fabric you select for these processes should not be stretchy or have a lot of give. They will stretch out when wet, and as a result the wax resist may crack.

OMBRÉ SCARF (detail). © Susan L. Moyer. *Here, layers of wax caught the loose dye as it was discharged, reflecting the application of one stroke of wax over another. Salt was used to create the textured background effect.*

RED BRUSHSTROKE SCARF. © Susan L. Moyer. *Both wax and Sennelier black gutta were used as resists here. The wax brushstrokes were placed over areas of the silk that were dyed red. The black gutta was then applied to section off other areas of color.*

OMBRÉ SCARF. © Susan L. Moyer. *The techniques used here are similar to those explained in the alcohol discharge demonstration on pages 114–115, except that the wax brushstrokes were applied over an ombré ground (a field of continual, solid colors that blend together from light to dark) rather than over separate areas of color.*

RED BRUSHSTROKE SCARF (detail). © Susan L. Moyer. *Between applications of wax, alcohol diluent was used to move the dye, creating drop-shadow effects.*

DEMONSTRATION:
Alcohol Discharge and Wax Resist Techniques

Alcohol helps make acid dyes very versatile and it can provide interesting and unusual effects, but you should remember to work in a well ventilated area with an exhaust fan when using it. The fumes can be overwhelming and dangerous.

To prepare the silk for the wet-on-wet technique illustrated here, stretch it tautly above your work surface, which should be protected with a plastic covering. Apply a diluent solution (of 50 percent water and 50 percent isopropyl alcohol) to the silk with a foam sponge brush. Don't overwet the fabric and create puddles though, because the dye will run into these spots and spread out of control. Blot the puddles and silk with paper towels before applying any dye.

In this photograph, dye is applied to the wet silk with an oval wash brush. Due to the alcohol diluent on the fabric, the shapes of color spread slowly, drying with a soft (rather than a sharp) edge.

While the silk is drying, melt the wax at 260° F. A mixture of 50 percent beeswax and 50 percent paraffin was used here. Temper the brushes in the melted wax, and execute a few practice strokes on newspaper. (Note: You will need a slightly lighter hand to get the same effect on silk.) Once the silk is dry, apply the wax over the color to be saved. Return the brush to the pan often to keep the wax on it hot and flowing; this will ensure that the wax penetrates the silk properly. (It should look shiny and clear, not dull and chalky.)

Now any dye that is not covered with wax is flushed (or discharged) out of the silk with alcohol diluent and a sponge brush. Place absorbent newspaper under the stretcher frame. Liberally apply the diluent to the fabric and dislodge the color by rubbing the silk with the tip of the brush. Flush the diluent and discharged dye from the silk in a circular motion, add more diluent, and repeat the process. Repeat until there is only a light halo of color left. This may take 8 to 16 ounces of diluent. (I used 8 ounces on the demonstration piece.) Remove the diluent-soaked newspaper, and let the silk dry until it is just damp.

Here dye is applied around the areas of wax resist using an absorbent oval wash brush that holds a lot of dye and comes to a good point (a squirrel-hair quill is another good choice). Overlap and blend areas of color as you do this, but be careful not to leave spots of dye on the wax. For this project, I also made use of the salt technique in which coarse, sea salt crystals are placed on top of the wet dye. The salt pulls the wet dye in various directions, creating a texture on the silk.

Drops of color that have formed on the wax can be removed with a damp cotton swab. Keep in mind that if they are not removed, they may penetrate the silk when the wax is ironed out or the dyes are steam-set.

Allow the silk to dry, and remove and discard the salt crystals. Excessive amounts of salt may attract moisture during the steaming process, causing water spots. Therefore, it is important to scrape off any salt residue that is visible to the eye.

I used both a foam brush and a Silver Econo gesso brush to apply the next layer of wax. I cut grooves into the ends of the foam to create the striped effect you see here. The foam holds a good amount of wax, enabling the application of long stripes, and the altered gesso brush creates the texture and feel of a light, dry brushstroke.

Another layer of dye (here, black) is now applied over the salt-textured ground colors. To obtain a rich black, allow the first application of dye to dry and then add a second coat.

When the painting is finished, all the wax must be removed from it. After the silk is dry, place it on a few layers of clean newsprint paper (approximately ¼-inch thick). Place two more sheets of clean newsprint paper on top of the painting. Using a hot iron on a dry setting, melt the wax into the paper.

Once the newsprint is saturated with wax, place the painting on fresh paper and repeat the process until only a light residue of wax is left in the painting. The painting is now ready for steam-fixing and dry cleaning (see chapter 9). Artists often bypass the ironing step because the wax can be removed during the steaming process; the wax melts off the fabric due to the steam heat.

8 SCREEN PRINTING

As you improve and grow as a silk painter, it becomes a challenge to discover new ways to express yourself. Professional artists often explore other surface design techniques and develop ways to make them compatible with the basic silk painting materials and techniques with which they are already familiar. One such artistic medium is screen printing, a process of making a print by pushing pigment through a stencil (or mask of some sort) and a fabric screen, resulting in an image on an underlying surface. Dye that has been thickened to a print paste consistency, as well as gutta and some water-based and water-soluble resists, can be screen printed onto silk.

My intent is to introduce the silk painter to a few basic screen printing processes that are compatible with the silk painting medium. Although the techniques covered should open the door to a wealth of creative possibilities, it is important to know that there are many more processes and technical aspects of screen printing that are beyond the scope of this book.

Untitled. © Kerr Grabowski

117

SCREENS

Screen printing processes, also referred to as silk screen (traditional screens were made with silk fabric), are used for many things. Images are screened onto T-shirts in mass quantities, but artists, perhaps most notably Andy Warhol, also use silk screen to create one-of-a-kind or limited-edition-series works of art. Warhol's silk-screened images of Campbell's soup cans and Marilyn Monroe are familiar to almost everyone.

This versatility provides many options: you can create a single print; a series of multiple, virtually identical images; or a series of similar images with slight alterations—a change in color, perhaps. The artist Kerr Grabowski, whose work is featured here, is constantly exploring the potential of the silk painting medium in relation to her own creative growth. For Kerr, as for all artists, the exploration of this intrinsic relationship is an informative and ever-challenging process. She uses screen printing in combination with other surface design techniques to create her unique fabrics and was very instrumental in assisting me in my experimentation with her screen printing techniques.

Fabrics

Multifilament polyester and less-expensive polyester curtain-sheer fabrics (in white) found at fabric stores and outlets make ideal screens when printing with water-based mediums. Finesse and Ninnon are brands of curtain-sheer fabrics that you might want to try. Multifilament fabrics are identified by a double-X system and range from 6XX (approximately 86 threads per inch) to 16XX (approximately 232 threads per inch). The fewer the number of threads per inch, the larger the openings between the fibers to allow the print medium (the pigment or resist used) to pass through. When using a water-based resist as her printing medium, Kerr opts for a 8XX or 10XX screen fabric (larger openings);

when using dyes as the medium, she prefers a 10XX or 12XX screen fabric (smaller openings).

When working with photographic stencils and solvent-based (or gutta) mediums (covered later in this chapter), a monofilament polyester fabric is better.

Frames

Frames can be constructed with four wooden bars or supports, which are sometimes referred to as balusters. Use two for length and two for the width. To determine the length of the frame bars, select your print size and add 2½ to 3 inches to both ends of each piece of wood. This extra length is an allowance for the wells. These are the borders of the screen, which are masked with tape to hold the print medium and provide a place to rest the squeegee (where it will not touch the screen) both before and after pulling a print. I recommend a wide well because it will better hold resists or dye mediums and prevent them from spreading onto your screen. This is especially true with gutta resists, which can be very runny. Preassembled frames can be purchased at art supply stores in standard sizes and fabrics. Others can be ordered to custom specifications from mail-order catalogues (see List of Suppliers).

Squeegees

Squeegees are used to force the print medium through the open areas on your screen. They are measured by inch widthwise and are composed of a wooden handle with a rubber blade. To adequately push the medium over the entire screen, the squeegee should extend ½ to 1 inch into the side wells when placed in the frame. The blades are available in various durometers (degrees of hardness), with 45 being extra soft and 80 bone hard. Soft to medium blades are recommended for printing onto

UNTITLED. © Kerr Grabowski. Photo by the artist. *Kerr's sophisticated color harmonies, spontaneous drawing, and sensuous textures are the result of a combination of various surface design techniques. She paints directly on the silk with liquid dyes and screen prints with resists, discharge pastes, and thickened dyes. The concentration of blue, yellow, and red hues contrasted against the black and white panels and borders make this a lively triad color scheme.*

SHARK FIN SOUP (front). © Kerr Grabowski. Photo by the artist. *To create her black-and-white designs, Kerr makes a print paste with sodium alginate (see pages 122–124) for her fiber-reactive dyes and then screen prints the medium using a variety of stencils. Some of the panels of this garment were executed with a wax resist technique and others by painting dye directly onto the silk without use of a resist. The contrasting panels were then sewn together to form unique, wearable art.*

SHARK FIN SOUP (back). © Kerr Grabowski. Photo by the artist. *Kerr used paper, wax, and photostencils to print the various panels. To create the subtle blue checked areas, she printed a thin layer of Inkodye resist on the white silk crepe and then painted on it with fiber-reactive dyes. The dye penetrated the thin layer of resist in varying degrees, creating shadowed images.*

textiles because they conform to the fabric's surface and therefore deposit more print medium on it. Finding the appropriate blade flexibility is usually a matter of experimentation, but a good starting durometer is 60 (a standard, medium weight). To support it so that it will not fall into the print medium, you can attach a dowel to each side of the squeegee (see the squeegee in the following demonstration). Take care not to nick the blade when storing your squeegees; a damaged blade may result in uneven distribution of the print medium on your fabric.

Screen Tape and Varnish

Wooden frames should be protected from moisture, otherwise they will warp. The wood can be carefully coated with polyurethane, and the inner sides and the wells should be covered with tape and sealed with a topcoat of shellac. A new and effective alternative is Screen Tape. It is made of polyester film and is very easy to use, because it doesn't need to be sealed and is easy to clean and apply. For the screen in the screen printing demonstration I covered the supports with duct tape and then used Screen Tape to mask the wells and reinforce the inner sides of the frames.

Print Boards

The silk screen print board is a sturdy, padded, lightweight, and inflexible supporting foundation over which the fabric or surface to be printed on (the print surface) is placed. It ensures an even print surface, resulting in good screen-to-fabric contact and thorough, even coverage of the print medium. Complete guidelines

for constructing your own print board are provided in Joy Stocksdale's book *Polychromatic Screen Printing,* but I've outlined the procedure here as well.

Basically, to build a padded print board you will need ½-inch thick dacron batting, sheets of 12- or 16-gauge plastic, muslin cloth, and the supporting, underlying board. One possible board material is a rigid, lightweight, foil-faced foamboard called Energy Shield, manufactured by Atlas Energy Product. You will also need duct tape and pins. To ensure that the screen maintains even contact with the silk on the print surface (and so that the frame doesn't rock when you pull a print), the minimum measurement for a print board should be 1 inch larger than the outside measurement of the screen frame.

To begin, cut a piece of foamboard to the desired print board size. Also cut a layer of batting to match this size. Place the batting over the foamboard and temporarily tack it in place with the pins; the pins should be positioned at least 1½ inches in from the edge and angled toward the center of the board. Then using the duct tape, attach the edges of the batting to the edges of the foamboard by placing half the width of the tape on the batting and pulling it tightly toward the edges before securing it. Make sure the surface is smooth, and remove the pins.

Now you are ready to cut the plastic. Cut it at least 4 or 5 inches larger than the board dimensions (so that you will be able to wrap it around the edges of both the board and the batting and secure it to the board's underside). Place the board upside down in the center of your cut piece of plastic. Pull the plastic over the back of the board and tack down the center of each edge. Then go back to secure these edges more thoroughly. To avoid ripples as you tape the plastic down, place strips of tape at 6-inch intervals (or less depending on the size of the board) on the edge of the plastic and use them to pull and stretch the plastic from the centers toward the corners so that it is taut and smooth on the print board surface. You should leave the corners for last, cut out any excess plastic (that can cause unwanted lumps), and tape down. Avoid creating any creases in the plastic because they will cause uneven textures in your design when the print medium is applied.

When printing, you will need to stretch a backcloth over the plastic and secure it with tape on the print board. The silk is then stretched onto the backcloth and attached with pins or tape. Traditionally, the backcloth is a piece of muslin, which will absorb the excess print medium as it seeps through the silk when a print is pulled. The backcloth is removed and washed between printings.

Screens, Print Boards, and the Moyer Design Fabric Stretching System

Traditionally, printing surfaces for mass-produced fabrics are large enough to accommodate printing repeats on yardage. A larger surface (such as a 4- by 8-foot Atlas Energy Shield) would also facilitate work on several small pieces of fabric so a series (or edition) of prints could be pulled at one time. For the silk painter who has limited space or who wants to produce monoprints (single, unique prints), print boards and screens can be coordinated in size with the Moyer Design Fabric Stretching System mentioned in Part I.

Once you have stretched your silk on the Moyer Design system, it does not need to be removed and restretched on the print board for use in screen printing, as with other, more conventional stretching methods. The fabric remains stretched on the frame throughout all of the silk painting and screen printing processes. For screening, the frame legs are removed and the frame (with the stretched silk) is placed on the print board and under the screen. The system ultimately saves time and space. If you are planning to do successive prints (a series), you will need to set up a frame for each print. The frames can even be stacked while the silk dries on them.

When using this fabric-stretching system for screens of up to 36 inches square, the print screen and print board should fit inside the inner perimeters of the system's stretcher frame (see the following demonstration). For example, if the inside measurement of the frame is 20½ inches square, the print board and screen should fit inside this length, leaving at least a ½- to 1-inch allowance for the metal loops and elastic that run along the inside of the fabric stretcher frame. The maximum outside measurement of the print screen and print board would then be 20 inches square.

Keep the following print screen frame calculations in mind as an example: A 20-inch-square screen frame constructed from 1-inch supports would include a screen area of 18 square inches. The screen will be further decreased 2½ to 3 inches on each side by the taped well, giving you an open print space of 12 or 13 inches square. Note that larger screens would require wider, 1½-inch supports.

The Moyer Design Fabric Stretching System has been developed to encourage experimentation in design and can be adapted so several techniques can be combined with screen printing to build up a composite design or monoprint (see following demonstration). However, I should point out that it is not designed for perfect registration (placement) when one stencil design is used repeatedly or is to be printed over another screened design.

When screen printing, you can increase stability and control the registration of the print by constructing a hinge bar on the screen that attaches to the stretcher frame, securing the fabric stretcher and print screen frame together. For the screen used in the following demonstration, the hinge bar is attached to the screen with two 2-inch split pin hinges and ¼-inch machine screws so that the print screen can be easily removed afterward. The depth of the hinge bar should be less than that of the supports so that the screen lies evenly when lowered onto the silk. A print can then be pulled without the screen shifting, affecting the registration.

STENCILS

Stencils function in a similar way to the resists used in other silk painting processes. Wherever the stencil covers the screen, the print medium will not penetrate to the silk below. They can be made from paper, wax, and even photographic and light-sensitive materials. Paper and wax stencils are less permanent, while photographic stencils are durable and fairly permanent once adhered to the screen fabric. For this reason, photostencils may be the better choice for the artist who is producing multiple prints of the same design.

Paper Stencils

Stencils can easily be cut or torn from paper. Freezer paper (used to wrap food for freezer storage) is a heavyweight, white paper similar to parchment, which works especially well because its coating prevents the stencil from becoming saturated with the print medium. You can cut or tear out shapes from a sheet of paper and use them as your stencils, or you can use the piece of paper from which they were cut. Either way, the paper stencil is arranged, coated side up, over the stretched silk, and the print screen is placed over it.

The print medium is poured into the well and is pulled across and through the screen onto the silk below using the squeegee. After the first print is pulled, the wet print medium holds the stencil in place on the screen, providing an opportunity to pull a few more prints. Once finished, remove the stencil and clean the screen before the medium has a chance to dry.

Wax Resist Stencils

Liquid hot wax and wax crayons can be applied directly onto the screen to create stencils. For the hot wax, use a mixture of 50 percent beeswax and 50 percent paraffin. It can be applied using a variety of implements, such as tjanting tools and brushes. Apply melted wax to the front of the screen, which should be raised off the work surface. After applying the wax, check the back side of the screen for wax drips. Any drips must be carefully removed with a blunt knife so that the screen maintains even, unbroken contact with the print surface.

Wax rubbings and drawings made on the screen with pieces of wax or wax crayons also make effective stencils. Choose a lightly colored crayon (rather than white) so that you can see it better against the screen fabric. Rub the crayon (or wax) into the

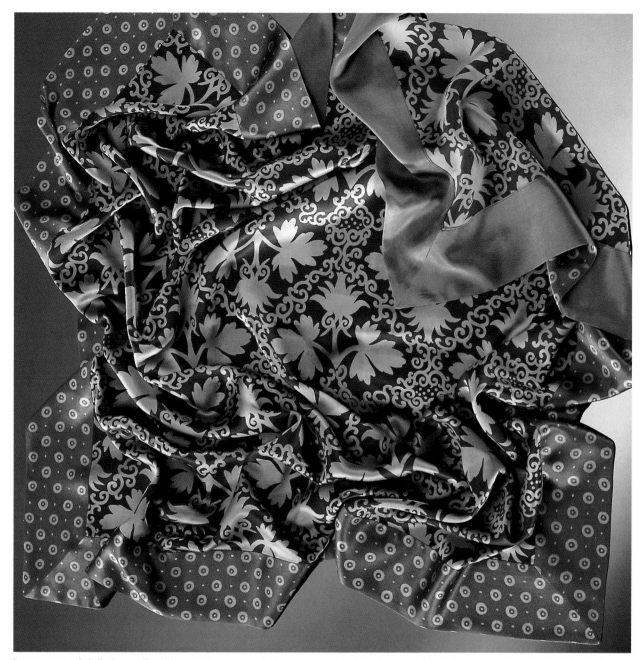

SQUARE SCARF. © Sally Jones. *For this and other scarves, Sally works on a beautiful, heavyweight silk charmeuse. To create her fabric designs she screen prints thickened dyes and discharge pastes over painted grounds.*

screen until the fibers are filled with wax. To set the wax in the screen, hold a dry, hot iron a few inches above the screen until the wax softens into the screen fibers. Don't heat the wax too much or it will melt through the screen fabric and not be an effective resist.

To clean a screen and wax stencil without removing the stencil, flush it with plenty of cold water. Avoid solvents, which will dissolve the wax, and hot water, which will melt it. To remove the stencil from the screen, place newspaper both on top of and underneath the screen. Iron over this with a warm (not hot) iron until the wax melts out of the screen. The newspaper will absorb the wax and help protect the polyester screen fabric from the direct heat. After ironing, remove any wax residue that may be left by rubbing the screen with a soft rag and a solvent, like Turpenoid or mineral spirits.

Photostencils

Photographic stencils are durable and stand up well to repeated use. Also called photostencils, they are made by placing light-sensitive film material against the screen fabric and exposing them to ultraviolet light. The light-sensitive film hardens on the screen creating a stencil.

The equipment and space (a darkroom is best) required for making these stencils is too extensive to cover in this book. But, you can have photo screens made at professional photo screen suppliers. Make sure you tell them which print medium you plan to use so that they use the appropriate film; water-based print mediums (such as the thickened dyes and H. Dupont Serti HPNO, discussed in the next section) require water-resistant stencils, while solvent-based print mediums (gutta) require solvent-resistant stencils. You must also supply them with a

OBLONG SCARF. © Sally Jones. *This is another example of Sally's rich designs. The coffee cup motif adds a feeling of whimsy to this oblong scarf.*

photographic positive of your design; this means that you simply execute the design in black on white paper. Ask the photo screen supplier if he will need a copy from a copy machine, a black-and-white stat, or a clear stat with the design in black.

There is also a thermal screen product that is similar to the photo screen process. It is a polyester screen fabric coated with a heat-sensitive plastic film emulsion. A stencil is made by placing an image (your design) against the screen emulsion and exposing it to an intense flash of light. The stencil is the result of the contact of the thermal screen coating with the carbon-based inks or carbon pencils used to draw your designs. Since heat imaging is used to create the stencil, no solvents or photography materials are required. This screen fabric is available in precut sizes or by the yard at some art supply stores (such as Pearl Paint in New York City) and can be ordered by catalogue from Welsh Products, Inc. (see List of Suppliers).

PRINT MEDIUMS

There are a number of methods for screen printing a design on silk. When using these print mediums in conjunction with the other silk painting processes in this book, you should make sure that all the dyes and silk types are compatible. One medium you can use is a mixture of dye and a print paste, which is printed directly onto the silk through the screen. Another technique is to screen a water- or solvent-based resist onto the silk; areas that receive the resist will resist any further applications of dye.

You can also experiment with mixtures of print paste and dye-discharging agents. When this is printed onto already painted silk, the agent will discharge the dyes, creating a lighter design on the fabric.

Print Pastes and Preparation

Both acid and fiber-reactive dyes can be thickened for use as print mediums in the screen printing technique. To thicken, combine them with either a manufacturer-prepared print paste or one that you make from sodium alginate. Sodium alginate (available from fabric art suppliers) is a nontoxic thickener made from seaweed that will not react adversely when mixed with dye. It is used in a granular form, which expands and thickens when mixed with water. The dyes are added to the print pastes after the alginate paste mixtures have been individually prepared.

Sodium alginates are of either the low-viscosity (LV) or high-viscosity (HV) type. Both can be used to create a print paste, but the low-viscosity variety is better for screen printing on silk because it consists of smaller particles, which can be more successfully squeegeed through a fine mesh for delicate line definition.

Sodium alginate itself does not sustain bacteria and will not grow mold, but the addition of water when making the print paste may promote bacterial growth. When a sodium alginate print paste ages, it will become thinner but may still be usable; just make sure it is not so thin that it seeps under the stencil

OBLONG SCARF. © Sally Jones. *Once Sally has completed her fabrics, she coordinates the patterns into panels for scarves. Each scarf is double-sided, and many of her luxurious scarves also have double-sided borders.*

during printing. To prolong its shelf life and retard spoilage, refrigerate the sodium alginate paste and, if you want, add a food preservative to it. When stored properly, the print paste should last up to three months. Always allow the paste to reach room temperature before using.

Print pastes that are to be made with liquid dyes should be mixed thicker than the pastes made with powdered dyes. The reason being that you must compensate for the additional liquid of the dye. For the most part, prepackaged liquid acid dyes do not require auxiliary chemicals for steam-fixing and can therefore be added to an alginate paste that is made only with water. (Fiber-reactive dyes used for making print pastes require additional chemicals.)

Powdered acid dyes, on the other hand, are not traditionally packaged with acid and so you must add white vinegar (which contains 5 percent acetic acid) to the paste mixture to lower the pH level to approximately 4. This will ensure the fixing and full richness of the colors. You should test the pH level of the paste prior to adding the dye, and you can do this with testing materials available through chemical suppliers. When mixing a print paste with powdered fiber-reactive dyes, you will need to add a manufacturer-recommended chemical water to the paste mixture to help the dye bond with the silk before and during the steam-fixing process.

To prepare approximately one quart of either type of print paste, you will need four cups of liquid, which will vary in

Recipes for Low-Viscosity and High-Viscosity Sodium Alginate Pastes

LV paste (yield: approximately 1 quart)

4 cups of the appropriate liquid

3¾ teaspoons sodium hexametaphosphate (the active ingredient in Calgon)

5 tablespoons sodium alginate LV for liquid (acid) dyes; 4–5 tablespoons for powdered dyes

Mix as instructed below and let sit for a minimum of 15 minutes (or overnight for a smoother consistency) in the storage container. Note that sodium hexametaphosphate is also in Calgon. Sodium hexametaphosphate is preferable, but Calgon is more common and may be easier to find.

HV paste (yield: approximately 1 quart)

4 cups of the appropriate liquid

2¼ teaspoons sodium hexametaphosphate

3 tablespoons sodium alginate HV for liquid dyes; 2–3 tablespoons for powdered dyes

Mix as instructed below and let sit overnight in the storage container.

composition, as specified here, according to which type of dye you plan to use. Note: When working with powdered dyes, wear a mask and rubber gloves for protection.

Prepackaged liquid acid dyes: 4 cups warm water, or slightly less if more concentrated color is desired

Powdered acid dyes: 1 tablespoon white vinegar plus enough warm water to equal a total of 4 cups

Powdered fiber-reactive dyes: 4 cups of the appropriate chemical water

You will also need the following equipment:

- a blender, or large plastic, glass, or stainless steel mixing bowl, and a spoon
- measuring spoons and cups (glass, stainless steel, or plastic)
- 2-quart plastic storage containers for the paste

Mixing the ingredients. Pour the four cups of warm water into the blender and add the sodium hexametaphosphate. With the blender on a low speed, slowly add the sodium alginate. Once the surface is no longer pulled under by the blending (about two minutes), pour the paste into the plastic container.

If you are mixing the print paste by hand, rather than using a blender, you may need another person to help you. Pour the four cups of warm water and the sodium hexametaphosphate into the large bowl. One person very slowly sprinkles the sodium alginate into the warm water, while the other rapidly stirs the mixture.

Checking the print paste consistency. When working with powdered dyes, check the consistency of the print paste before adding the dye. For liquid dyes, check the paste consistency after adding the dye.

To check consistency, spoon up a large scoop of print paste and let it drip off the spoon. The print paste should flow in a steady stream. If the paste is too thick, it will break and not flow easily or evenly. To thin it out before adding powdered dyes, add a bit more water. To thin it out when using liquid dyes add more liquid dye. When adding ingredients, add only a little at a time and test frequently. The paste should be slightly thicker than honey.

Adding dye to the print paste. It is easier to mix a deep, rich color from the concentrated powders than it is from liquid dyes, which are really intended for painting directly on the silk. When making a print paste out of liquid dyes, take care that the mixture does not become too liquidy. One way to compensate for this is to prepare a thicker print paste by adding less water to the alginate.

Acid dye powders should first be made into a slight paste with a small amount of boiling or very hot water. Slowly add more boiling water until the powder is completely dissolved. The mixture should be allowed to cool to room temperature and then added to the print paste. For a medium shade, start with ½ teaspoon of dye to 1 tablespoon water per 4 cups of print paste. You may find that a few powdered acid dye colors are difficult to dissolve. Try adding a little bit of urea to the cooled solution to help dissolve any stubborn dyes. Urea is a powdered solubilizing agent available through chemical suppliers. It will decompose at high temperatures, so don't add it to boiling or very hot water.

Test your shades by smearing the colored print paste on a scrap of silk. When adding highly acidic colors to the print paste, the pH level may become too low causing the alginate to break down and curdle. On the rare occasion that this happens, add an acid donor (ammonium sulfate or ammonium oxalate salts available through chemical suppliers) to the print paste to increase the acid content. It won't change the chemistry of the dye but will prevent the acid from reacting with the alginate.

When dissolving powdered fiber-reactive dyes, the optimum temperature for the mixture depends upon which type of dye is being used. MX-range fiber-reactive dyes need 75- to 95-degree water, while H-range dyes can withstand hotter temperatures. Neither should be dissolved in boiling water.

Gutta Resist

Clear gutta can be used as a treatment on both unpainted and painted grounds. Screening the gutta treatment onto the silk

THE AVIARY (detail). 1978. © Jane Herzenberg Design Studio. *Early in her professional career, Jane produced a collection of designs by screen printing her gutta resist. Here you see an example of a linear resist motif that was printed over a light yellow ground and then painted.*

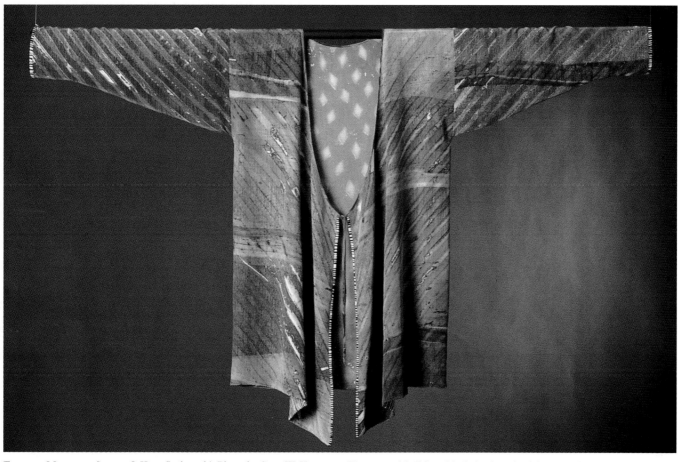

THUNDER MOUNTAIN SWAMP. © Kerr Grabowski. Photo by Sean W. Hennessy. *Kerr started building this design by using leftover yardage from a previous project. She painted directly over this fabric with fiber-reactive dyes and created the highlights with Presist, which was applied to select areas to discharge the color.*

through a paper stencil design creates a lot of interesting possibilities. After it is applied, dyes will move and flow easily on the untreated areas of the fabric, but will not flow when painted on the treated parts. On these treated areas, you will be able to paint clearly-defined brushstrokes and create shapes that will not disperse on the silk.

The sticky gutta must be thinned with Turpenoid or mineral spirits so that it can be pulled through the open mesh with the squeegee. You will need to experiment to find a printable consistency that still maintains a good resist. Start with a mixture of 80 percent gutta to 20 percent solvent, and, if necessary, thin it down a 60:40 ratio. The gutta will be runny and difficult to control in a narrow screen well. A wider 2½- to 3-inch well may prevent the liquid from overflowing onto the silk. Depending on the weight of the silk, you may need to pull the gutta across the screen twice to penetrate its fibers. The fumes from the gutta treatment are strong so work in a well-ventilated area. Whenever possible, let the prints dry outside.

To clean, place the screen on a stack of newspapers. Wear rubber gloves and rub the screen with a soft rag saturated with Turpenoid or mineral spirits. Change the paper as it absorbs the gutta and solvent. The solvent is highly flammable so exercise caution when using it. Do not store solvent-soaked materials in your studio; let them dry outdoors.

Water-Based and Water-Soluble Resists

H. Dupont has developed a water-based screen printing resist for production art called Serti HPNO. It is an acrylic-like substance and is hard and permanent once it dries on the silk. Since it cannot be washed or dry-cleaned out and has a stiff texture, its use should be limited to open linear patterns (rather than solid, dense shapes) in order to preserve the soft drape of the fabric. Despite this limitation, it does have some unique features. It can be screened in a linear design over a painted ground and tinted with dye to impart a colored resist line.

Inkodye and Presist are other water-soluble resists that offer successful screening results when working with both acid and fiber-reactive dyes. If using acid dyes, do not use alcohol diluent; water-based resists are not as durable as gutta and wax and will break down easily when used with alcohol. The water-soluble resists are screened onto silk (similar to gutta resist), and both wash out in warm water after steam-fixing. As with all water-based resists, the Presist will discharge (partially remove) the previously unfixed ground colors over which it is printed, leaving a hint of any underlying color. Once the resist is applied, the silk is steam-set and the resist is removed, taking with it some of the underlying unset color. This characteristic creates subtle highlights when painted or screened onto already painted silk. Inkodye will also discharge color but not as much as Presist.

DEMONSTRATION:
Screen Printing with Gutta Treatment

In the following demonstration, I use the Moyer Design Fabric Stretching System to illustrate screen printing and gutta resist treatment techniques. This is the general procedure for screen printing, which you can adapt to any print medium. Just keep in mind that you must prepare your screen appropriately to accommodate either water- or solvent-based print mediums.

To prepare a ground to screen, I have stretched the silk on the Moyer Design frame, which is raised above the work surface on its removable legs. For the ground seen here, I first applied a wash of alcohol diluent to the fabric to achieve softer brushstrokes and deter the dye from striking the silk. Then I painted the design using a combination of wet and dry brush techniques and let it dry thoroughly. Other painting techniques that can be used to decorate printing grounds are: ombré (the gradual blending of one color into another), line building (using the line edges formed by dye washes to create designs), and salt. Gutta treatment printed on white silk can also result in some exciting possibilities.

After the silk has dried, I remove the frame legs from the stretcher, attach the screen and hinge bar over the frame, and place the print board underneath. To hold the screen in position while printing, I use a flat T-plate (like those used for industrial bracing) and a ¼-inch machine screw (1 inch long). For protection, the sharp corners of the T-plate have been covered with duct tape. To prop up the screen (as in the next picture), you can attach a thin piece of wood to the side of the screen.

Here I arrange a paper stencil made from freezer paper cut-outs on the fabric, coated side facing up toward the screen.

You should always lower the print frame at this point to check the position of the stencil pieces. If satisfied, turn the T-Plate to secure the screen.

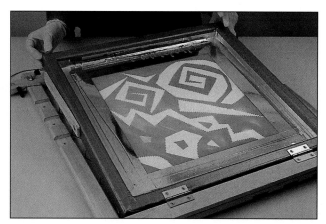

For this project, I used gutta treatment (thinned gutta) for the print medium. Pour the medium into the top screen well and pull it toward you to the bottom of the screen with the squeegee. You should use both hands for this, and hold the squeegee at about a 45-degree angle to the screen. The angle of the squeegee will determine the amount of print medium deposited on the silk: the larger the angle, the thinner the deposit; the smaller the angle, the thicker the deposit. To prevent drips on the screen after a pull, pull all the print medium entirely into the bottom well, and keep the squeegee off the mesh when not in use. It is best to only pull the ink over the screen once because repeat pulls may cause the stencil to shift, disturbing the print registration.

Immediately after printing, remove the stretcher frame with the printed fabric from the print board, reattach the legs (as in the following photograph), and allow the silk to dry. Also keep in mind that once one print has been pulled, the print medium will keep the paper stencil adhered to the screen, enabling you to pull a few additional prints. (Any fabric necessary for multiple printings must be stretched and prepared for printing beforehand.)

Once you have completed the printing, use a rubber spatula to scrape off any unused print medium. Save this for reuse. Remove the stencil and clean the screen thoroughly with the appropriate solvent.

Screen printed gutta treatment gives the silk painter some exciting creative options. Since the dye will move easily on the untreated areas (those that were covered by the stencil), these spots can be filled in with flowing color. Here I fill one untreated section with dye, which flows up to the edges of the treatment and then stops. Dye can also be painted on the areas of gutta treatment (the spots that were not covered by the stencil), but it will not move as it does on untreated areas. This is because the treatment controls the dye flow. Each brushstroke will remain visible and clearly defined, and the results will look similar to painting with watercolor on paper.

9 PRACTICAL CONSIDERATIONS

Once your silk painting or garment is complete, you are ready for the finishing process. Proper finishing techniques give your work integrity and the respect it deserves. Steam fixing and framing increases the presence of your artwork and imbues it with a finished quality that sets it off from its surroundings. It is very rewarding to see one of your compositions mounted and framed or to wear a beautiful handpainted silk scarf or tie. Your skill and creativity should be proudly showcased.

When finishing your work, you must consider both the time-tested methods and the materials used so that you can best extend the life of these creations. Setting the dyes in the fabric properly and framing and caring for the silks in a way that promotes longevity will ensure lasting enjoyment.

MURAL IN THE ELEPHANT BAR AT THE EAST 21 HOTEL IN TOKYO (details).
© Antoinette von Grone

STEAM FIXING

The steaming process not only sets the dye permanently and bonds it with the silk, but also develops the color to bring out all its brightness and intensity. Once the dyes are fixed, your silk creations can be washed or dry-cleaned. (Note that silks containing metallic gutta and some pigmented resists should not be dry-cleaned; follow setting instructions on product packaging.) During steaming, heat and moisture penetrate the dyes to create a concentrated dye bath, which sets the dye. Pébéo Soie, Tinfix, Super Tinfix, H. Dupont, and Jacquard Red Label Silk Color dyes all require steam fixing. The Jacquard Green Label Silk Colors dyes are immersed in a premixed dye setting solution to set them and develop their full color. Steaming will also remove some of the wax resists used in the painting processes, and any residues still remaining in the silk will be removed when the silk is dry-cleaned. After the dry cleaning, the silk is rinsed in a bath of clear water to remove any excess dye.

Steaming equipment can be purchased, or simple household items can be used to assemble a steamer, like the canning pot used in the following demonstration. A large stove pipe steamer can also be assembled for steaming yardage. This is a large galvanized stovepipe (which can be purchased at local plumbing and heating supplier) placed over a heavyweight cooking pot filled with a few inches of water. The paper-wrapped silk is then hung into the pipe, suspended above the water by a hanger. A cover of newspapers and towels seals off the top to keep the steam inside the pipe. For more information on assembling this economical steamer please refer to *Silk Painting: The Artist's Guide to Gutta and Wax Resist Techniques.*

Preparing the Silk

Before steaming, the painted fabric is first wrapped in newsprint (or in a fine muslin cloth and newsprint) and then rolled in a covering of kraft paper. (Moving supply companies are a good source for inexpensive packing newsprint paper that can be purchased by the pound.) All the paper used for steaming should be uncoated and porous so that steam can penetrate through the roll or bundle to reach the silk during the fixing process. (See the demonstration for actual rolling instructions.)

Paper is fine for silks with resists that are to be removed (such as clear gutta) because, as mentioned above, these substances will be dry-cleaned out of the fabric later. Paper also absorbs some of the wax resists, eliminating the need to iron the wax out prior to steaming. (If there is a heavier layer of wax, some of it should be ironed out of the silk first.) However, a layer of muslin is more appropriate for wrapping silks containing resists that will remain in the fabric (black or metallic gutta). The muslin can be pulled free of these stickier resists more easily than paper. It is then washed and reused. Paper has a tendency to tear and stick to a tacky resist, and this will ruin your artwork.

Steaming

Depending on the thickness of your rolled silk, the fabric should remain in the steamer for 2 to 3 hours. For wearable art, 4 hours is recommended. I have found that a canning pot, with its inside supporting rack, makes a successful steamer. I wrap the cover in newspapers and a towel to absorb excess moisture.

You should check the water level periodically and refill the pot with boiling water if necessary. Do not let the pot boil dry or your silk will discolor or, even worse, turn to ashes. You might find putting a penny in the water to be helpful; you will hear it rattling around as long as there is still water in the pot. When you no longer hear it, it's time to refill. A loud timer that can be carried with you if you leave the room will also help you avoid a silk-burning disaster. (Note: If you regulate the heat source to maintain a simmer and the lid is secured tightly, chances are the water will not boil away and you won't need to add more during the steaming process.)

When the steaming time is up and the heat is turned off, immediately remove the package from the steamer, unroll it, and allow the silk to air dry. If the kraft paper is not damaged, it can be reused.

Storing the Pot

Once a pot has been used for steam fixing, it should not be used for food preparation. After the steaming process is complete, remove the canning rack and save the circular newspaper padding (see demonstration). Clean the pot, and let the damp padding and assembled lid (towel and padding) air dry so they can be reused. Once dry, the rack and padding can be stored in the clean pot.

DRY CLEANING

After the silk has been steamed, it should be dry-cleaned to remove any remaining gutta or wax. Dry cleaning is a textile-cleaning process that uses solvents instead of water. There are a variety of solvents that can be used; common ones are benzene, naphtha, and perchloroethylene, a solvent often used by professional dry cleaners. Dry cleaning solvents require special handling and, oftentimes, permits for their use and disposal. So, while you could dry-clean your work yourself, it is probably best to keep personal health and environmental awareness in mind and use a professional dry-cleaning service. There are bulk dry-cleaning businesses, often located in local laundromats, which charge by the pound or load. Even if your silks weigh much less than the maximum weight per load (which is usually approximately 8 to 10 pounds), bulk dry cleaning will still be more economical than dry cleaning per piece.

RINSING, IRONING, AND CLEANING

Once the dyes have been steam-fixed and the silk dry-cleaned, the fabric should be rinsed in water to remove any excess dye, chemicals, or salt residue, and restore the natural pH level. For optimum bonding of the dye to the fabric fibers, wait 48 hours after steaming fixing before rinsing the silk. Rinse it in a tub of lukewarm water (70 to 90°F). (Professional silk painters often add Synthrapol to the rinse to remove loose dye and deter backstaining.) Use plenty of water so that it can circulate completely around the silk and wear rubber gloves to protect your skin from any discharged chemicals. Do not twist or wring the silk, and do not let dark areas touch light areas for any length of time. Repeat this rinse process two to three times. To neutralize any traces of alkali, the next to last rinse should include a bit of white vinegar (use one tablespoon per quart of water).

Wearable art that was executed with black or metallic gutta and that does not require dry cleaning to remove gutta or wax should also be rinsed in water to remove excess dye and restore

DEMONSTRATION: Steam Fixing

To prepare the package of rolled silk and paper (or cloth), lay a large sheet of kraft paper on a clean, flat surface. Place 2 layers of newsprint paper (or 1 layer of muslin) on top of the kraft paper. Place your fabric on top of these layers leaving a 2-inch border of newsprint on all sides, and cover with 2 more layers of newsprint (or 1 layer of muslin). Before and during rolling, smooth out the fabric so that wrinkles do not occur during steaming. To protect your fabric from condensation, the kraft paper should extend beyond the ends of the newsprint enough so that the rolled layers of silk and newsprint are enclosed in 3 to 5 layers of kraft paper.

If you are steaming more than one layer of silk, place 2 layers of paper (or 1 layer of muslin) between each layer of painted fabric, ending with a layer of paper (or muslin) on top. Pieces of painted fabric can be put next to one another, but they should not overlap. Loosely roll the layers together, and as you do this, smooth out any creases in the fabric. Keep the ends of the roll even, and tape the roll securely.

Coil the roll and secure it with string or heavy-duty rubber bands.

Use a canning pot for the steamer. To assemble it, first pad the lid. Cut a pile of newspaper (⅜- to ½-inch thick) into a circle that fits inside the lid. Lay the paper on a thick cotton towel, and place the lid over it. Gather the sides of the towel up and fasten securely over the top of the lid.

Invert the canning rack and place it in the bottom of the pot. Fill the pot with approximately 1 inch of water. The water level should be at least 2 inches below the top of the rack so that the boiling water doesn't splash onto the rolled package. To further protect the package from any splashes or condensation, place more circular layers of newspaper (⅜- to ½-inch thick) on the rack. Also layer 1 circular sheet of aluminum foil in the middle of this pile of newspaper. Once the water is boiling, position the silk package on the paper-padded rack. Check that both the package and newspaper pad are not touching the sides of the pot. Also make sure that the lid and padded towel clear the top of the package.

To prevent a possible fire, give the towel a final inspection to ensure that it will not hang or slip over the sides of the pot. Once the water is boiling and the lid is on the pot, adjust the heat sources so that it maintains an even, constant simmer.

the silk's natural softness and pliancy. Repeat the rinsing process described above until the water runs fairly clear, and again do not twist or wring the fabric, or leave in a heap.

After rinsing, roll the silk in a clean towel to remove excess water and hang (or lay flat on top of a towel) to dry. You can iron the fabric while still damp to better remove wrinkles. Ironing silk while it's damp gives it a pleasantly soft hand and also increases the richness of the colors. Redampen if necessary. Set the iron on the synthetics/steam setting. Place a press cloth or tissue paper on top of the silk to prevent leaving iron marks on your designs and always iron on the wrong side. Black and metallic guttas will smear on the silk and iron so always put tissue paper over and underneath the fabric while ironing. Replace the tissue paper as soon as it becomes soiled so that it does not restain the silk.

For general washing of soiled silks, hand wash in lukewarm water with a mild soap like Ivory Liquid or Liquid Tide. Never use harsh detergents or bleach. Most garments constructed out of painted silks, which have been properly steam-set and rinsed, are hand-washable, but delicate, highly constructed garments should be dry-cleaned to maintain their shape.

FRAMING ARTWORK EXECUTED ON SILK

Framing is an art form in and of itself. It requires superb aesthetic judgment and craftsmanship. The function of a frame is to protect and visually separate a piece of art from its surroundings; but it shouldn't be so noticeable that it distracts from the artwork. The frame should highlight and encourage the viewer to focus on your silk painting. The quality of the framing job conveys an artist's professional integrity and respect for his work and audience. The type of frame selected is a reflection of personal taste and style, and can even be the result of a collaboration between the artist and the client.

Professional framers often use a mat (a border around the artwork) as an additional means of setting the artwork off from its surroundings. When mounting artwork under glass, the mat (usually a heavy cardboard) also prevents the silk from coming into contact with the glass (or clear Plexiglas—acrylic plastic sheets) and any condensation (from the air) that might collect on its underside. The mat can also be integrated with the design, becoming part of the artwork itself. For example, sometimes artists Linda and David Hartge cover their mats with painted silk. The pattern of the mat silk complements the patterns in the artwork. However, whatever style you choose, frame and art should form a cohesive unit.

Protecting Silk Under Glass

Paintings are often framed behind glass to protect them from dirt, dust, and grease (from cooking and fingerprints). The backs of the frames are sealed with a backing board or paper. Since part of the beauty of silk painting is the tactile quality of the fabric, many artists find it difficult to put their work behind glass. They lament that a layer of glass physically and psychologically separates the viewer from the work, preventing intimate contact with the sensual qualities of the textile.

If, after careful consideration, you decide the artwork should be behind glass, there are a few options available to you. Conservation nonglare glass, or a clear acrylic-like Plexiglas or

---

Should I Use Glass?

To help you decide whether or not to use glass, consider these practical issues:

- As a rule, silk paintings should be kept out of direct sunlight. Heat and sun destroy silk fibers and fade dyes. Ask yourself to what environmental elements the painting will be exposed, other than direct sunlight; glass may help protect against excessive moisture and dirt. Also keep in mind the projected life span of the artwork; glass may help extend it.

- Where will the painting be hung? Will it be displayed in a gallery, shop, art show, office building, restaurant, or private home? If the artwork is to hang in a restaurant, glass will help protect it from harsh elements such as smoke and grease. If the piece is intended for a less-trafficked bedroom, one might be less inclined to use glass so that the sensual qualities of the fabric can be fully appreciated and experienced.

---

styrene, filters out ultraviolet rays and cuts down on reflection and glare. Dyes will be protected from both ultraviolet and indirect sunlight, which may also cause colors to fade. Sheets of acrylic are not as fragile or as heavy as glass, making them an excellent alternative when framing artwork that will travel. However, acrylic does scratch easily and should be cleaned with a nonabrasive cloth and clear spray wax or soapy water. Do *not* use traditional cleansers or glass cleaners, which will cause the acrylic to cloud or become foggy.

Unlike many other materials, silk is a natural fiber and needs to breathe. Therefore, when mounting silk under glass, make sure that air is still able to circulate around the fabric. One way to ensure proper ventilation is to punch a few small holes in the backing paper before taping it to the frame. Professional framers use a hole punch to keep the holes neat.

Planning for Successful Artwork

Before beginning a silk painting, you will need to consider the characteristics of your chosen fabrics. Determine which stretching technique will be most suitable for your silk and will ensure that the finished work can be properly mounted and framed. Plan ahead; if you do not, you may end up with unsatisfactory results. It may take a little experimentation and a few compromises before you find the compatible materials and techniques that work best for you.

Many silk painters prefer to work with crepe fabric because, unlike habutai, it can be stapled (to a frame) without developing pulls and runs. Also, the resilient and flexible quality of the crepe weave enables it to adjust for stress points on the frame over which it will be stretched and tacked down. These stress points, which tend to develop and become more apparent over time, are more visible in the plain, woven fabrics. They are also less noticeable on crepes because this silk is not as shiny as other varieties and, therefore, is less likely to reflect any stress spots.

Stretching Techniques

Traditionally, tapestries and delicate fabrics were stretched and mounted by being laced around a board or some other flat sur-

MENDOCINO. © Natashe Foucault. *This painting has been wrap-stretched over wooden stretcher bars.*

Planning Tips

- *Design.* Consider your design in relation to your framing technique. For example, an image with a straight-edged border painted on a stretchy fabric will be difficult to stretch for framing. If you are not careful as you stretch the fabric, the border may also stretch unevenly. To prevent this and make the stretching job easier, make sure that any straight border lines in your design follow the grain of the fabric so that they are not pulled out of shape. Another alternative is to avoid painting straight borders on your composition. Many interesting borders make use of abstract shapes and wavy lines.

- *Measurements.* Fabrics can shrink in length up to 2 inches per yard during the steaming, dry-cleaning, and rinsing processes. If you are not prewashing your fabric, you may want to factor in extra length when measuring the silk for a project. Also, add a 2-inch border around a painting for ease in handling and tacking down the silk during the stretching process.

- *Stretcher bars.* Lightweight canvas stretcher bars are an inexpensive support for displaying silk paintings. The painting is stretched over and wrapped around this wooden support frame, as in the demonstration later in this chapter. Also called wrap-stretching, this solution eliminates the need for a frame. If you are planning to use the wrap-stretch technique, you must increase the planned dimensions of your design by about 2 inches so that the silk can be wrapped around the back of the frame without distorting the image.

CACTUS. © Roberta Glidden. Photo by the artist. *The rich colors in this composition were brought out even more by the steam-fixing process.*

face. But double-sided acid-free tape and the staple gun have both made contemporary stretching and framing projects much easier. Artist Roberta Glidden stretches and staples her paintings over an acid-free foamcore board, which she first covers with a layer of thin, white polyester batting. This technique is suitable for both heavyweight and delicate, lightweight silks.

Other artists use double-sided tape instead of staples to mount their paintings on acid-free foamcore. A double-sided, acid-free needlework tape is available from United Mfrs. Suppliers, Inc. To use, measure and cut tape to desired length and adhere one side of it onto the foamcore. Then remove the shiny protective paper covering to expose the adhesive on the other side. You can now position and adhere the fabric on the tape. For larger paintings, you might also want to reinforce the tape by stapling the silk through it onto the foamcore at 1-inch intervals.

Artist Suzanne Punch stretches her large, abstract paintings executed on medium- to heavyweight crepe de chine over lightweight canvas stretcher bar frames that have first been covered with a stretched piece of white cotton flannel. The flannel gives the silk body and helps protect the delicate fabric from the bare wooden stretcher bars. It also prevents the bars from showing through thinner silks, disturbing the paintings. Once her paintings are stretched, Suzanne slips them into simple, precut, metal sectional frames without mats or glass.

Another option is a self-adhesive, acid-free mounting foam and boards manufactured by Pres-On Merchandising Corp. This product was originally developed for mounting needlework, and it can be useful when making craft projects, such as fabric-covered albums, journals, and ornaments. It is also effective for mounting paintings executed on medium- to heavyweight silks. According to the manufacturer's instructions included in the package, any fabric that is mounted on this adhesive board is repositionable for up to 30 minutes (or until the adhesive dries). This is a plus if you don't get the mounting position quite right on the first try. The manufacturer also says that paintings executed on a durable silk can later be lifted off the adhesive for cleaning and then remounted. These Pres-On boards are available in crafts stores in sizes up to 32 by 40 inches.

A note of caution: I have spoken to silk painters who, on the advice of professional framers, have had their work professionally laminated with heat-sensitive adhesives to foamcore or acid-free board for framing. After several years or a sudden change in humidity and temperature, bubbles have formed under the silk. This is partially due to the natural expanding and contracting of the fabric. Some lamination and mounting processes may be permanent, so the fabric cannot be removed for cleaning and then reattached. Keep this in mind if you choose a mounting technique like this.

STRETCHING SILK OVER CANVAS STRETCHER BARS

In the following demonstration, I stretched a painting over lightweight canvas stretcher bars like those mentioned previously. The dyes in your artwork should be set, and the silk should be thoroughly washed. The fabric doesn't necessarily need to be ironed, though, because the stretching process will pull it smooth. The stretcher bars must be unwarped, so check this before you purchase them. If your bars are longer than

MOZART SOIREE. © Antoinette von Grone. *As with the silk painting on the previous page, the colors of this composition were enhanced by the steaming process.*

44 inches, you should reinforce the frame with a crossbar.

If you are planning to frame your painting after it is stretched, select a frame that is made with a deep enough rabbet (groove) to accommodate the depth of the stretcher bars, and any glass, mat, and backing board you might be using.

Materials

4 lightweight canvas stretcher bars

4 right-angle corner clamps

right angle

polyurethane and brush

glue (make sure it will work on wood)

sandpaper

¾-inch acid-free framer's tape

double-sided, acid-fee adhesive tape

white cotton flannel (washed and rinsed well)

ruler and tape measure

mat knife

scissors

staple gun and fine, rustproof staples with a ¼-inch tack point (depth)

staple remover

small hammer

4 to 8 pushpins

dressmaker's marking pencil

clean water in a spray bottle

kraft paper

hair drier

picture hanger

DEMONSTRATION: Stretching Your Silk Painting

In this wrap-stretch method for displaying a painting that will not be framed, the artwork is stapled to the back of the stretcher bar frame. For work that is to be framed, the painting is stapled to the sides of the stretcher bar frame, and the excess fabric is trimmed off.

A day or so before you plan to stretch your silk, prepare the stretcher bar frame by sealing the wood with a coat of polyurethane. This will keep the chemically-treated wood from discoloring and eroding the fabric. Let the bars dry thoroughly and then set the frame in corner clamps. Use the right angle to establish a 90-degree angle at each corner. One corner at a time, release the clamp, glue the bars together with wood glue, and reclamp. Double-check your angles, and let the glue dry thoroughly. Remove the clamps, and sand the corners and edges to eliminate any rough spots or bumps that might catch the silk or distort the painting's surface.

Stretch your artwork (right side down) tautly on a clean work surface and tack the edges down with four strips of acid-free framer's tape or masking tape. Position the stretcher frame over the fabric. Using a dressmaker's pencil, put a mark on the center of the inner side of each bar and place corresponding marks on the back of the artwork. Also mark the placement of the frame's corners on the back of the silk. Measure the depth of the stretcher bar frame (in this case, ⅝ inch) and add ⅛ inch to that. Draw a border on the fabric around the frame at a distance from the bars that is equal to this measurement (here, ¾ inch). (For artwork that is to be stapled to the stretcher bar sides, not the back, draw a line next to the frame.) As in the photograph, apply strips of ¾-inch acid-free framer's tape to this line, stopping 2 inches in from each corner. (The tape will prevent the staples from creating pulls in the fabric, and will later act as a guide for stretching and positioning the silk on the frame.) Now remove the tape that is holding the silk to the work surface. The silk may ripple a bit; this is to be expected.

Cut a piece of flannel to cover the frame. Each side should equal the corresponding bar length plus an extra 4 inches. Stretch the flannel onto the frame, and, using a staple gun, place one staple through the fabric in the center of each bar. Also put a temporary staple through the fabric in each corner.

Staple each side from the center to within 3 inches of each corner. Do one side and then its opposite. While doing this tacking, keep the grain of the fabric straight, and place the staples at a slight angle to avoid weakening the fabric.

Use the staple remover to carefully remove the temporary corner staples.

Pull and stretch the fabric away from the corners, easing the fabric into soft gathers. Smooth out any wrinkles in the flannel on the sides of the frame. If the wrinkles are stubborn, remove a few staples and rework the fabric until the flannel lies flat against the frame, and restaple. Smooth, neat corners are very important, especially in an unframed wrap-stretch.

Staple the corners securely over the frame. Use a small hammer to lightly tap any protruding staples into the wood.

Using the positioning marks drawn earlier, place the flannel-covered frame onto the back of the artwork. Stretch the silk onto the back of the bars so that the tape is approximately ⅛ to ¼-inch in from the inside edge of the frame. (Note that the acid-free tape is not removed. It is under the silk so you don't see it.) Press the silk into place. Secure with one pushpin in the center of each side.

Flip the painting over and dampen the front with water. Make sure you keep the water away from any tape. Keeping the silk damp, stretch and staple the painting exactly as you did the flannel. The staples should be placed through both the silk and the underlying tape at a slight angle. Use the tape as your guide, and work from the center of each bar to within 3 inches of each corner.

Pull and stretch the corner fabric until it is smooth. You may need to carefully remove and restaple a few spots. At this point, you should hang the painting for a few days to be sure that no sagging or unevenness develops. If it does, remove a few more staples and readjust the silk. Again, lightly tap any protruding staples into the wood. (If you have stapled the silk to the sides of the stretcher frame and if the painting is to be framed with glass and backing materials, you may need to trim off any excess fabric that is creating too much bulk for the rabbet.)

To back a wrap-stretched painting, cut a piece of heavy kraft paper that is approximately ⅛ inch smaller (all around) than the framed piece. Adhere it to the back of the frame with double-sided tape.

For a more professional-looking framing job, wet the backing paper by evenly misting or sponging it with water.

Dry the backing paper thoroughly using a hair drier. As the paper dries and becomes taut, push down on the strip of tape so that the paper does not pull loose.

To attach the picture hanger, find the center on the back of the top bar of the painting. (The one pictured here is an adjustable Moore sawtooth picture hanger.) Place the hanger near the lower edge of the bar, making sure that it is parallel to the top edge, and lightly mark this placement with pencil. Hammer the nails (that come with the hanger) through the hanger into the back of the stretcher bar frame.

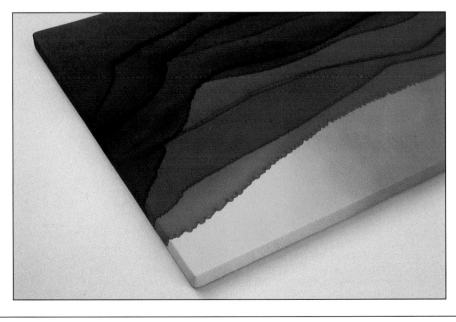

The stretched, wrapped painting is ready to be hung.

LIST OF SUPPLIERS AND MAIL-ORDER CATALOGUES

ALJO Manufacturing Co.
81-83 Franklin Street
New York, NY 10013
(212) 226-2878
(212) 966-4046
FAX (212) 274-9616
powdered acid and fiber-reactive
dyes and related chemicals

Artisans Textiles
9 Hall Place
Albany, NY 12210
(518) 434-8946
Dye Tech 60 machine

Atelier de Paris
Showroom:
1543 S. Robertson Boulevard
Los Angeles, CA 90035
Mailing Address:
1556 S. Fairfax Ave.
Los Angeles, CA 90019
(310) 553-6636
FAX (310) 931-7474
importers of H. Dupont dyes
and related products
silk, steaming service,
workshops

**Design Inspiration
Bookshop, Inc.**
488 Seventh Avenue, 12C
New York, NY 10018
(212) 736-1537
FAX (212) 465-1134
color and trend information,
books, international magazine
subscriptions

Dharma Trading Co.
P.O. Box 150916
San Rafael, CA 94915
(800) 542-5227
(415) 456-7657
FAX (415) 456-8747
H. Dupont, Sennelier Tinfix and
Super Tinfix, and Jacquard dyes
and related products;
fiber-reactive dyes; silk

Exotic Silks
1959 Leghorn
Mountain View, CA 94043
(415) 965-7760
(800) 845-SILK outside CA
(800) 345-SILK in CA
FAX (415) 965-0712
silk

Galerie Smend
Mainzer Strasse 31
50678 Cologne
Germany
(0221) 31 20 47
FAX (0221) 32 51 34
H. Dupont, Sennelier Tinfix
and Super Tinfix, and Uhlig
dyes and related products;
German books on silk painting;
silk; workshops

Hobbidee
Turbinenmstrasse 7
Postfach 31 12 53
7000 Stuttgart 31
Germany
(0711) 8 30 86 0
FAX (0711) 8 38 05 97
H. Dupont dyes and related
products, silk

Horikoshi New York
55 West 39th Street
New York, NY 10018
(212) 354-0133
FAX (212) 354-2971
fine Japanese silk, wool challis
•may have minimun order
requirement; call for
appointment

**John Marshall: Works
in Fabric**
2422 East 23rd Street
Oakland, CA 94601
(510) 533-8056
FAX (510) 533-8056
Japanese brushes, shinshi

Maiwa Handprints
6-1666 Johnston Street
Vancouver, B.C.
Canada V6H 3S2
(604) 669-3939
FAX (604) 669-0609
Pébéo Soie and fiber-reactive
dyes and related products,
print screens, print pastes,
related chemicals,
Japanese brushes, shinshi,
silk

**Moyer Design & Silk
Painting**
P.O. Box 98
Ridgewood, NJ 07451-0098
for orders:
(800) 780-6377
please send all other inquiries to
above address or fax:
FAX (201) 652-7779
Moyer Design Fabric Stretching
System, Susan Louise Moyer
Brush Sets, Susan Louise Moyer
Pébéo Dye Sets and Kits, Pébéo
Soie dyes and related products,
books, private lessons,
international workshops

**New York Central Art
Supply Company**
62 Third Avenue
New York, NY 10003
(212) 477-0400
(800) 950-6111 outside NY
FAX (212) 475-2513
H. Dupont and Sennelier Tinfix
and Super Tinfix dyes and
related products

Pearl Paint
308 Canal Street
New York, NY 10013
(212) 431-7932
(800) 221-6845
FAX (212) 431-5420
Jacquard and Sennelier Tinfix
and Super Tinfix dyes and
related products, brushes,
Japanese Riso Mesh (thermal
emulsion screens) and
related materials

PRO Chemical and Dye, Inc.
P.O. Box 14
Somerset, MA 02726
(508) 676-3838
(800) 2-Buy-Dye
FAX (508) 676-3980
Pébéo Soie and fiber-reactive
dyes and related products,
Susan Louise Moyer Pébéo Dye
Sets and Kits, print paste materi-
als and all related chemicals,
seminars

Qualin International, Inc.
P.O. Box 31145
San Francisco, CA 94131
(415) 333-8500
FAX (415) 282-8789
H. Dupont, Sennelier Tinfix and
Super Tinfix, and Jacquard dyes
and related products; silk; work-
shops

Rupert, Gibbon and Spider, Inc.
P.O. Box 425
Healdsburg, CA 95448
(800) 442-0455
(707) 433-9577
FAX (707) 433-4906
wholesale/retail
Jacquard products, silk,
steamers

Savoir Faire (Importers of Fine Materials for the Arts)
P.O. Box 2021
Sausalito, CA 94966
(800) 332-4660
FAX (800) 299-3113
importers of Sennelier products
Sennelier Tinfix and Super
Tinfix dyes, squirrel-hair quill
brushes, related silk painting
products
• will provide list of retail stores

The Shepherdess
2802 Juan Street
San Diego, CA 92110
(619) 297-4110
FAX (619) 297-9897
Pébéo Soie and H. Dupont dyes,
workshops

Shop Text
10-12, rue Taylor
75010 Paris
France
(1) 42 49 05 22
FAX (1) 42 49 18 73
Pébéo Soie and Javana dyes and
related products, silk, books,
brushes

Silkcraft
75 Coniston Road
Dronfield Woodhouse
Sheffield, S18 5PZ
England
FAX (01246) 290179
H. Dupont dyes and related
products, silk, steaming service

Silkpaint Corporation
P.O. Box 18
18220 Waldron Drive
Waldron, MO 64092
(816) 891-7774
FAX (816) 891-7775
and
47-194 Kamehameha
Highway
Kaneohe, HI 96744
(808) 239-9299
H. Dupont dyes and
related products,
Silkpaint Air Pen

Sureway Trading Enterprises
826 Pine Avenue, Suite 5
Niagara Falls, NY 14301-1806
(716) 282-4887
FAX (716) 282- 8211
H. Dupont and Sennelier Tinfix
and Super Tinfix dyes and
related products, silk

Testfabrics
P.O. Box 420
Middlesex, NJ 08846
(908) 469-6446
FAX (908) 469-1147
degummed, scoured, and
bleached silk and wool (ready
for painting)

Thai Silks
252 State Street
Los Altos, CA 94022
(415) 948-8611
(800) 722-SILK outside CA
(800) 221-SILK in CA
FAX (415) 948-3426
silk

Ulano Corporation
255 Butler Street
Brooklyn, NY 11217
(718) 622-5200
photo screen printing materials,
screens made to order

United Mfrs. Supplies, Inc.
1701 Clint Moore Road
Boca Raton, FL 33487
(800) 645-7260
FAX (516) 496-7968
and
80 Gordon Drive
Syosset, NY 11791
(800) 645-7260
FAX (516) 496-7968
framing equipment, acid-free
tape, and other products

Wildfiber
1453-E 14th Street
Santa Monica, CA 90404
(310) 458-2748
H. Dupont and Jacquard dyes
and related products, silk,
fiber-reactive dyes,
workshops

Wolfmark Neckwear
133 N Jefferson, 6th floor
Chicago, IL 60661
(312) 715-0511
(800) 621-3435
FAX (312) 715-0514
will make ties and scarves from
your painted silk yardage

SUGGESTED READING

Bristow, Nicholas. *Screen Printing: Design and Technique.* London: B. T. Batsford Ltd, 1990.

Brown, Gail. *Sensational Silk: A Handbook for Sewing Silk and Silk-like Fabrics.* Portland: Palmer/Pletsch Associates, 1982.

Faine, Brad. *The Complete Guide to Screen Printing.* Cincinnati: North Light Books, 1993.

Hargrave, Harriet. *Mastering Machine Appliqué: The Satin Stitch.* Lafayette, California: C&T Publishing, 1991.

Joyce, Carol. *Textile Design: The Complete Guide to Printed Textiles for Apparel and Home Furnishing.* New York: Watson-Guptill Publications, 1993.

Kolander, Cheryl. *A Silk Worker's Notebook.* Loveland, Colorado: Interweave Press, Inc., 1985.

Meller, Susan, and Joost Elffers. *Textile Designs: Two Hundred Years of European and American Patterns for Printed Fabrics Organized by Motif, Style, Color, Layout, and Period.* New York: Harry N. Abrams, Inc., 1991.

Quiller, Stephen. *Color Choices: Making Color Sense Out of Color Theory.* New York: Watson-Guptill Publications, 1989.

Schwalbach, Mathilda V., and James A. Schwalbach. *Screen-Process Printing: For the Serigrapher & Textile Designer.* New York: Van Nostrand Reinhold Company, 1970.

Stocksdale, Joy. *Polychromatic Screen Printing.* Berkeley: Oregon Street Press, 1984.

Townswick, Jane. *Quiltmaking Tips and Techniques: Over 1,000 Creative Ideas to Make Your Quiltmaking Quicker, Easier and a Lot More Fun.* Emmaus, Pennsylvania: Rodale Press, Inc., 1994.

INDEX

POPPIES. © Linda France Hartge and David Hartge. *In this painting, two images from nature are used as contrasting elements. The poppy plant naturally creates strong upward movement that is enhanced by the vertical format of the composition. The diagonal lines created by the bending iris leaves contrast this motion, while the bold primary colors (also found in nature) add life and drama to the work.*